THE
NORTH RIVER

THE
NORTH RIVER

SCENIC WATERWAY OF THE SOUTH SHORE

JOHN GALLUZZO

Charleston   London

History
PRESS

Published by The History Press
Charleston, SC 29403
www.historypress.net

Copyright © 2008 by John Galluzzo
All rights reserved

All images courtesy of the author unless otherwise noted.

First published 2008

Manufactured in the United Kingdom

ISBN 978.1.59629.222.2

Library of Congress Cataloging-in-Publication Data

Galluzzo, John.
The North River : scenic waterway of the South Shore / John Galluzzo.
p. cm.
Includes bibliographical references.
ISBN 978-1-59629-222-2 (alk. paper)
1. North River (Plymouth County, Mass.)--History. 2. North River Region (Plymouth County, Mass.)--History, Local. 3. Historic sites--Massachusetts--North River Region (Plymouth County) 4. Parks--Massachusetts--North River Region (Plymouth County) 5. Natural areas--Massachusetts--North River Region (Plymouth County) 6. Natural history--Massachusetts--North River Region (Plymouth County) 7. Wild and scenic rivers--Massachusetts--Plymouth County. I. Title.
F72.P7G25 2008
974.4'82--dc22
                              2007050742

To Professor R. Dean Ware, who once told me that the weather in the Middle Ages was up in the air, and to Professor Franklin Wickwire, who gave me five extra credit points for suggesting that Walter Brennan should have played King John in Errol Flynn's Robin Hood.

CONTENTS

ACKNOWLEDGEMENTS

I've lived and worked my entire life on the South Shore, save for a brief four-year foray to Western Massachusetts to wrestle a bachelor's degree in history from the University of Massachusetts at Amherst and a two-year stay in Fairfield, Connecticut, for a job fresh out of college.

Other than that, the South Shore has been it. I grew up in Hull and Hingham, where my mother and father grew up, respectively. I have both of them to thank for helping to shape who I am today. I spent innumerable hours as a teen and beyond walking behind the lawnmowers of my father's landscaping company, gaining an appreciation for all things outdoors. We even cut a few lawns overlooking the North River from time to time, and at those times, reading some of the historical markers placed along the banks in the early 1900s, I let my mind wander. My mother's insatiable thirst for knowledge fueled my own, and her habit of taking us all—my sister Julie and my brother Nick included—to museums, parks and scenic vistas during the summer as kids made me unafraid of becoming classified as a geek for doing so on my own in my later years. My wife Michelle, as usual, has been very understanding as I have sleepwalked my way toward another book deadline. Thanks, Sweetie.

My real immersion in North River history (pun intended, sadly) came when I began work as the special projects coordinator (later executive director) for the Scituate Historical Society in 1999. David Ball and Fred Freitas, authors of so many important works on the town's history, were hard at work the year previous to that one preparing for the centennial anniversary of the Portland Gale of 1898. That event, of course, significantly impacted the North River story. I had studied the storm from afar, way up in Hull, where Joshua James and his boys had saved twenty lives. The centennial events—a postal cancellation at the Scituate Maritime & Irish Mossing Museum, the dedication of the Keeper Frederick Stanley Bridge and a plaque at Sand Hills to the memory of the crew of the pilot boat *Columbia*—opened my eyes to the bigger picture of the storm. Dave and Fred led me to the important works on the history of the river, allowed me to help in the interpretation of the society's standout maritime museum and let me live in two really cool places, the Little Red Schoolhouse on Cudworth Road and the Old Oaken Bucket House.

ACKNOWLEDGEMENTS

Many other Scituate residents and historians, including Carol and Paul Miles, Tom Hall and David Corbin, have guided me down the path to understanding the history of their community.

Across Little's Bridge in Marshfield, I've had the pleasure of working with Cynthia Krusell on a coauthored history of that town. Using the term coauthoring, though, in this instance, is like saying that David Ortiz (thirty-five) and Bobby Kielty (one) had a combined thirty-six home runs for the Red Sox in 2007. Cynthia is, by far, the Big Papi of Marshfield history research. Her work has set us all up for life with regard to knowing that community's history. Marshfield geographer Reed Stewart's work on the coastal geology surrounding the mouth of the North River has helped me understand its past, and even its future.

David Clapp, former director of Mass Audubon's South Shore Sanctuaries, gave me a chance to become a naturalist. Some day, maybe, it'll happen. In the meantime, the opportunity to work for Mass Audubon has allowed me the chance to explore the North River and its history—both from the North River Wildlife Sanctuary and elsewhere—at my own pace. David Ludlow, the longtime property manager of the South Shore Sanctuaries, has taken me down trails and dusty back roads to the hidden vistas and open spaces along the river, sharing his knowledge of their ecological management as far back as his family's memory goes. Ellyn Einhorn and I shared occasional lunchtime walks at the North River Wildlife Sanctuary, and at those times I picked her brain about the natural world around us, from ground covers on up. Years ago, another member of the Mass Audubon team, Wayne Petersen, answered the millions of questions I had about scoter ducks, the unwilling participants in the ancient South Shore art of making coot stews. Thankfully, he is now never more than an e-mail away when the world's birds conspire to confuse me. Sue MacCallum, the new South Shore Sanctuaries director, and Dianne Bartley have helped me understand the history of the building and grounds of the North River Wildlife Sanctuary, and the lives of the "ladies" who lived there for so long.

Other Mass Audubon staffers, including Andrea Jones, Ellen Jedrey, Becky Harris and particularly those with the Coastal Waterbird Program, have worked hard to protect the river and its fragile habitats. Samantha Woods, Paula Christie and the rest of the staff and board of the North and South Rivers Watershed Association fight that fight every day, encouraging citizen participation in monitoring projects, lobbying for the removal of dams and for laws minimizing and hopefully, someday, ending chemical runoff into the watershed, and the rivers are much the better for their presence and efforts. I'm honored to know them. Martha Twigg, a fellow Hullonian (yes, that's what someone from Hull is called), has taken the South Shore Natural Science Center to new places and heights, and is introducing a new generation of youngsters to the beauty of the North River and its tributaries. Judy Grecco of the North River Commission, a descendant of Cornet Robert Stetson, lent me some background material early in the process of the production of this book that has proved invaluable. Allan Holbrook, an alternate member of the commission; Jeff Ripley, keeper of the history of the Brick-kiln Yard; and Andrew Sullivan have all helped me understand a little bit more about the river and its glory days.

My desire for knowledge of the history of the United States Life-Saving Service has led to a secondary career as a sometimes-paid U.S. Coast Guard historian. Dozens of people around the country—especially Maurice Gibbs of Nantucket; Dick Boonisar of South Dennis; Ralph Shanks of Novato, California; Fred Stonehouse of Marquette, Michigan; and Dennis Noble of Sequim, Washington—have aided me along the way.

Several portions of this book have appeared in other forms in magazines and newspapers. I'd like to thank Alice Coyle, formerly of the *Scituate* and *Marshfield Mariners*, Rick Eggleston of *Northeast Boating* (formerly *Offshore*), Mary Grauerholz at *Cape Cod Life*, Susan Ovans at the *Hull Times* and especially Jaci Conry at *South Shore Living* for allowing me opportunities to tell the stories of local history for wide audiences.

In a weird twist, I'd like to thank Dr. George Snook, the surgeon who repaired my severely sprained left ankle in 1992. Once I got back on my feet—after spraining my right foot in a car accident while wearing the cast on my left—I had to teach my legs to walk again. I did that by visiting the Norris Reservation in Norwell and Wompatuck State Park in Hingham on numerous occasions, gaining more respect for nature each day as I walked the great Massachusetts outdoors.

As always, I have my UMass friends to thank. Professor R. Dean Ware and the late Professor Franklin Wickwire, to whom this book is dedicated, showed me the way toward quenching that thirst for knowledge of which I spoke, and showed me that I could have fun doing it. And now, a decade and a half beyond graduation, I am gaining new friends at the UMass History Department, Julia Sandy-Bailey and Professor Anne Broadbridge, and the many history majors I've had the pleasure to meet in recent trips "back home."

George Kerr, my best bud, must be mentioned and thanked with every book that I write. Go Sox, go Curt, go Papa G!

Finally, I'd like to thank the little people, Fred Morin and Mark Schmidt. If you're nice to me, there'll be new sponges and buckets for both of you guys next time you see me.

None of these wonderful people have anything to do with any errors in this book. Blame me, not them.

INTRODUCTION

There is no standard, all-encompassing view of the North River, except for, technically perhaps, one taken from the air. Yet, even with such a vantage point, the story of the river in its entirety cannot be fully discerned.

Altogether the North River flows about twenty-three miles to the sea (about ten as the crow flies), with the last six and a half miles or so passing through tidal marshes and estuaries as the river meanders out into Massachusetts Bay. That meandering characteristic of the river's ancient chosen path is the main reason that there is no one way to see the North River. It twists and it turns, offering one stunning natural vista after another. Whether traveling up- or downriver by canoe or kayak, crossing the river on one of the many bridges that transect it or simply walking along the trails of one of the numerous preserves, sanctuaries or other open spaces that line its banks, one can never gain a full appreciation of the beauty of the waterway and watershed. Even so, the one statistic about the river of which its protectors are most proud is that its collective beauty, the sum total of all of the vistas taken from all of the river's wanderings, made it the first designated Scenic River in Massachusetts history. It's also a Natural History Landmark.

There are statistics about the river that are, for many, unfathomable (no pun intended). The North River flows through five towns that rest about thirty miles south of Boston—Pembroke, Hanover, Norwell, Scituate and Marshfield—and its watershed stretches out to seven more: Hingham, Whitman, Duxbury, Weymouth, Rockland, Abington and Hanson. The watershed, meaning all of the waters that drain into the river as well as the main body itself, encompasses approximately 123,000 square miles, or 79,000 acres. That statistic includes the entirety of the South River, most of which was once part of the North River, until the Portland Gale of 1898 helped the larger river change its course. But we'll get to that story later on.

Ah yes, history. Therein lies another reason that there is no simple way to see the river from any single perspective. Like any place on the planet, the North River has meant many things to many users. The earliest European settlers saw it as a power source for mills, a provider of salt marsh for feed for cattle, thatch for roofs and insulation for houses. Soon thereafter they saw it as a place where ships could be built and, in 1800, for the

Gundalows were once the most prominent boats on the North River. The one seen here is piled high with hay on the left. *Courtesy of Historical Research Associates.*

only time in its history, this perhaps was the true singular meaning of "North River," the one thing that came to mind when anybody mentioned those two little capitalized words. The river and its surrounding lands were a fishery, a highway, a place of experimentation with oyster beds and cosmic rays, a military outpost and, sadly, a place of death. Sense of place is wholly dependent on the eye of the beholder. As the waters keep moving, constantly and dynamically changing, so too does the story of the river.

In this book you will meet Cornet Robert Stetson, an English immigrant who fought off an Indian attack during King Philip's War while in his sixties, and Jules Aarons, a scientist who studied the ionosphere from the Fourth Cliff Military Reservation. Walter Hatch will settle Two Mile thanks to Timothy Hatherly, the North River Boat Club will come and go and William Vassall will plant oysters in the muddy banks of the river. William Barstow will build a bridge, piping plovers will run for their lives from unexpectedly high tides on the Spit and Jeff Corwin will have something to say about how children on the South Shore learn about the natural world of the North River salt marshes.

One group of people you will not meet in depth is the Native Americans who lived on the North River Valley lands before European settlers arrived. The reasons for that fact are twofold. One, the study of Native Americans on the river deserves to be in a book by itself; and two, I am not currently qualified to write that book. I hope that someday a thorough work on the local tribes can be published, as that history is as fascinating as anything you will read in this book.

Today, the river is home to both pleasure and work craft.

The one thing that we all must remember when we study the story of the North River is that the river does not belong to any one community. Marshfield has no more right to claim it than does Norwell, and Scituate can't take it away from Hanover. That fact was never more tangible than during the heyday of North River shipbuilding. The young, talented shipbuilders who eventually left to find work in other yards along the coast were not known as Pembroke men or Scituate men; they were North River men. Ships built here were not Marshfield ships; they were North River ships. The people of the North River petitioned for changes that would positively affect them all, and not the men of one town over another. Rather than giving up its identity to any singular community, the North River was a community unto itself.

Historically speaking, the community continues. Timothy Hatherly, Walter Hatch, William Barstow, as well as Captain George Little, Timothy Williamson and even Jeff Corwin are all parts of the historical North River community. Each one has changed the course of the river's history in some small way, the collective sum of their efforts creating the North River we know today.

Luckily, there are scores of dedicated citizens living and working in the region today who are thinking as much about the future of the North and South Rivers as they are its past. In this book, we'll meet them, too.

Hopefully, by the time you're done reading these pages, you'll want to join them.

From the earliest days of New World settlement, history has been accumulating along the banks of the North River.

As It Was:
The View from 1831

Almost two centuries ago, the Reverend Samuel Deane of Scituate began work on a major history of his hometown, and why not? In 1836, the town would be two hundred years old. Bicentennials are big things, as those of us who lived through 1976 know.

As the North River played a major role in the life of the average Scituate resident to that point, much more so than it does today, the author penned a brief sketch of the river as it was at that time. What follows is his narrative, followed by only a few words from the current author:

"North River," from Samuel L. Deane's History of Scituate, 1831

This stream received its name before 1633, and probably from the circumstance that its general course is from south to north, or that it was farther from Plymouth than South River in Marshfield, which meets the North River at its mouth. The North River is a very winding stream, flowing through extensive marshes, sometimes, as it were, sporting in the broad meadows in the most fanciful meanders, and sometimes shooting away to the highlands which border the meadows. There is one reach which has long been called the "no gains" from the circumstance, that, after flowing from side to side, and almost turning backwards for several times, it has in fact flowed several miles, and gained but a few rods in its direct progress to the sea. From the sea to the North River bridge on the Plymouth road, an air line would not exceed seven miles: while the line of the Rover amounts to eighteen miles.

The tide rises at the North River bridge from three to five feet: and there is a perceptible tide two miles higher up. It has three chief sources, the Namatakeese and Indian head, which flow from the Matakeeset Ponds in Pembroke, and the Drinkwater, which has its sources chiefly in Abington. The tributaries are the three Herring brooks on the Scituate side and the Two Mile brook and the Rogers brook on the Marshfield side. Wherever the River in its windings, touches the highlands, there is a ship-yard, a landing or a fishing station. To name them in order, we observe that just by the bridge on the Plymouth road, is a ship-yard, which has been improved as such since 1699, Daniel Turner having been the first builder there that has come to our knowledge. A few rods below, on the Scituate side is a ship-yard, first improved by the Barstows in 1690. Just below the third Herring brook, and scarce a mile below the bridge, on the Scituate side, is a ship-yard, first improved by the Palmers and Churches, as early as 1690: now by Messrs. Copeland and Ford. Nearly opposite on the Pembroke side, at "the brickkilns" so called, is a ship-yard, which has long been used by the Turners and Briggses. Nearly a mile below this on the Pembroke side is "Job's landing," so called from Job Randall jr., who we believe resided near the place. A little below on the Scituate side are "Cornet's rocks" in front of the ancient residence of Cornet Robert Stetson. A half mile below on the Marshfield side is "gravelly beach," a principal station for the herring fishery and we believe vessels have formerly been built here. A little below, and at an air-line distance of two miles nearly from North River bridge above named, is the ancient Wanton ship-yard, used by that family in 1660, and subsequently by the Stetsons, Delanos and Fosters. Here the largest ships have been built, and more in number probably than at any other station on the River. A half mile (or something less) below on the Scituate side, is the ancient ship-yard of Job Randall, used by him about 1690; and subsequently by the Prouteys, the Chittendens and Torreys; and now by Messrs. Souther and Cudworth. A half mile lower on the Scituate side, is the "block house" where was a fort and a garrison in Philip's war. Here is a wharf and a ship-yard, which has been improved by the Jameses and Tildens for a century. Just above are "sunken rocks" on which vessels sometimes touch and are impeded. Just below, and at an air-line distance of a little more than three miles from North River bridge, is Union bridge. A half mile lower on the Scituate side, is King's landing. And about another half mile, on the same side, is Hobart's landing. Here we believe the first vessels were built, by Samuel House, as early as 1650; and soon after by Thomas Nichols: then by Israel Hobart in 1677; by Jeremiah and Walter Hatch soon after. The family of Briggs also have built vessels here for near a century, and it is still improved by the latter family, Messrs. Cushing and Henry Briggs. Here the Ship Columbia, *(Capt. Kendrick), was built by James Briggs, A.D. 1773. It was the first ship that visited the North West coast from this country. Capt. Kendrick explored the River Orregon, and named it from the name of his ship, which name will probably prevail henceforth. At the distance of another half miles below, is Little's bridge: at which point, we believe vessels have been built on the Marshfield side. The meadows above this station are of very various width, in a few places exceeding a mile: but below, there is a wide expanse of marsh, anciently called the "New Harbour marshes." The scenery here is on a sublime scale, when viewed from Colman's hills, or from the fourth cliff. The broad marshes are surrounded by a distant theatre of hills, and the River expands and embraces many islands in its bosom. Here it approaches the sea, as if to burst through the beach, but turns almost at right angles to the East, and runs parallel with the sea shore, for nearly three miles before it finds its out-let, leaving a beach next the sea of twenty rods width, composed chiefly of round and polished pebbles, excepting only the fourth cliff, a half mile in length, which comprises many acres of excellent arable land. Nearly a mile above the river's mouth, is White's ferry, where is a wharf and a small village on the Marshfield side. Here vessels have been built, and many that have been built above, here received their rigging. The river's width may be estimated as follows in ordinary tides: at Union bridge seven rods—at King's landing eight rods—at Little's bridge nine rods: it expands below to a half mile in width, where it is now called fourth cliff bay, formerly "New Harbour:" Here the channel divides, and unites again a mile below: a half mile above its mouth it is fourteen rods in width. The channel at the mouth often shifts its place, owing to the nature of the sandy bottom, and to the violence of the stream and the tides is but one channel: but it often happens that there are two channels when the water is something less. This fact accounts upon this river: and yet only in part, for there are shoals above, over which vessels of 200 tons and upwards must be lifted with gondolas or heaved with kedges. The principal are Will's shoal at the upper part of the New harbour marshes, and the Horse shoe shoal.*

Formerly, it is said, salmon were taken in this river. Bass had been abundant until within a few years: they are taken chiefly in winter. Shad and alewives are still taken, but they are gradually diminishing.

Deane's bird's-eye view of the river is rich in descriptive quality (his one error is that Captain William Gray navigated the *Columbia* up the river now named for it, not Captain John Kendrick, who became ill and switched commands with Gray and the *Lady Washington* before Gray made the journey), but is sad in one respect. His use of the past tense in 1831 when speaking of shipbuilding on the North River is surprising. We tend to think of shipbuilding ending in 1871 with the launch of the *Helen M. Foster*, and have a notion in our heads of an industry having to halt on a dime, stopped cold by a sudden lack of resources, among other factors. But the fact is that the real life of the North River was already vanishing by Samuel Deane's time. Shipbuilding had already peaked and was in steady decline, and the best shipbuilders of the North River were moving away from the corridor that from 1794 to 1804 had turned out an amazing 115 ships.

By 1831, Scituate, which until that time encompassed most of the lands surrounding the North River, certainly had a history.

STETSON MEADOWS

The title is composed of just two words, one standing for colonial history and the other for nature. But, aside from crumbling stone walls, there is little left today to remind the visitor to this Norwell open space parcel of the man who first settled the land and left it his name.

We know plenty of details about the men and women who escaped religious persecution and sailed the *Mayflower* across the Atlantic in 1620 to carve out a new life in the North American wilderness. In fact, we have what almost amounts to a colonial history theme park dedicated to them in the fabled town of Plymouth, to the south of the river. Yet our historical interest in the seventeenth century seems to stop there, save for a fascination with witchcraft and persecution on the North Shore of Massachusetts (and yes, in Scituate). We don't seem to pay nearly as much attention to the people who came to the New World shortly after the Pilgrims' arrival, on the *Mary and John*, the *Lyon* and others. Yet these folks, who set up the communities of Wessagussett (Weymouth), Naumkeag (Salem) and others, played roles just as important in the formation of the character of Massachusetts as those played by the settlers at "Plimoth."

Robert Stetson, an English settler who arrived in Scituate some time after 1634, was one such person. Stetson, born in 1613 and married to Honour Tucker in St. George's Church in Modbury, Devon, joined numerous others leaving the country in the days preceding the outbreak of the English civil war. King Charles I, the son of James I (also known as James VI of Scotland), caused ripples of concern to spread throughout England when he married Henrietta-Marie de Bourbon, a French Catholic princess, shortly after he ascended to the throne in 1625. King Henry VIII had created the Church of England less than a hundred years earlier, for his own selfish reasons, and it had become the religion of choice for the people of that nation, leading to decades of turmoil between Protestants and Catholics that often wrought bloodshed. During the reign of James I (1603–1625), the three countries of the British Isles finally found peace, but the possibility that the next generation of potential monarchs could be raised as Catholics set the populace on edge.

Moreover, Charles yearned to insert England into wars on the European continent and, as such, needed the support of Parliament to raise sufficient funds to do so. A botched continental expedition in 1627 led Parliament to begin impeachment proceedings to oust

Dragonflies like the common whitetail can be seen in open spaces like Stetson Meadows.

the Duke of Buckingham, the expedition's leader and the favorite of the king. Charles countered by dissolving the sitting Parliament and calling a new one the following year to raise the money he needed. He then set out on a period of more than a decade of rule without any Parliamentary input. During this time, young Robert Stetson immigrated to his new home. The move came none too soon; two early battles of the English civil war would be fought in his hometown of Modbury, in 1642 and 1643.

The Colony Court deeded Stetson forty acres on the Scituate side of the North River in 1634, but genealogists disagree on when exactly he and Honour arrived in the New World. One child, a son named Urith, was baptized in Plymouth, England, in 1636, and a second son, Joseph, was born in Scituate in 1640. Robert swore to the Oath of Fidelity in Scituate in 1642, being elected a constable the following year. A roll of men of Scituate able to bear arms in 1643 shows his name, and the role of soldier is one that he would eventually play. Stetson's life is remembered as a long and productive one, rather than for one act of bravery on a battlefield or a single moment of entrepreneurialism.

Stetson sold his farm in 1651, yet remained in Scituate. He achieved freeman status in 1652, and served his first term as the town's representative to the General Court in 1654. In total, he served for seventeen years as the representative, on nonconsecutive occasions, serving his last term in 1678.

Deer are among the many visitors to Stetson Meadows.

In 1656, he answered the community's call for "any man or men of the town to set up a saw mill upon the third herring brook as near the North River as conveniently it may be," with several provisions. The miller would be paid 50 percent of the wood he cut, provided he cut all of the timber of the townsfolk before he cut his own. Also, should there be no timber to saw to keep the mill busy, the miller would have the "liberty to make use of any timber upon the common to saw for their benefit." Harnessing the power of nature, Stetson built a water-powered sawmill on Third Herring Brook that stood for almost twenty years, providing a valuable and necessary service to the local citizenry. In 1662, he sold out his one-third financial interest in the mill to Joseph Tilden, stating that the mill had been built by Stetson, Tilden and Tilden's stepfather, Timothy Hatherly. This mill may have been the first sawmill in the New World.

In 1673, the town recognized that the mill's best days were behind it, passing the following act:

> *Whereas it is apprehended that the saw mill upon the 3d herring brooke will not stand longe, and when it is downe, the millpond will be the occasion of miring of many Cattell, for the preventing of which, and that improvement may be made thereof for meadow, it is agreed and concluded that when the saw mill is down, and seases to be a mill there,*

that then the mill pond shall be divided unto the now proprietors of the Towne, or their successors, and by them to whom division is made, to be well and sufficiently fenced.

Stetson continued to serve his community in important ways. He earned the title cornet while serving as the standard bearer of one of the Massachusetts Bay Colony's first cavalry units in the late 1650s. The rank of cornet, third in line below captain and lieutenant in the English military hierarchy of the time, and therefore the lowest commissioned rank in the cavalry, would evolve into second lieutenant in 1871. In 1658 or 1659, he sat on the colony's council of war. In 1664, he helped lay out the boundary between the Plymouth and Massachusetts Bay Colonies, and from 1665 or 1666 to 1671, Stetson served his hometown as selectman.

Past his sixtieth birthday, he saw his first military action. Tasked with brokering a peace between the Wampanoag chieftain Metacomet, also known as King Philip, Stetson and a band of other negotiators headed out for Mount Hope, the sachem's seat in Rhode Island. Diplomacy failed, and war began. On April 21, 1676, raiders attacked Scituate. "It was repulsed by the townsmen," wrote Harvey Hunter Pratt in *The Early Planters of Scituate*, "led by Isaac Chittenden and Cornet Robert Stetson, an Indian fighter of no mean abilities and then sixty-four years old." On May 20, 1676, Native Americans again attacked Scituate, burning nineteen houses and destroying the sawmill Stetson had built two decades earlier (at which time the above-mentioned act went into effect). The Englishmen, against a largely superior force, wrote Pratt, "encouraged by the venerable Stetson and Isaac Chittenden who was later killed in the fight, held the red terrors at a distance while the latter burned their dwellings, destroyed their cattle and newly planted fields, and then returned to the fight." The Scituate men retreated to a garrison house at the millpond at Greenbush (today known as Old Oaken Bucket Pond) and held off the attackers until sundown, when the natives disengaged from the battle and left town.

By 1678, Stetson had removed himself from public life, "retiring," as much as anybody in seventeenth-century America could do so, around age sixty-five. Surrounded by a large family (Honour died in 1684, and he remarried), wealthy in both coin and land, Stetson lived until 1702, dictating his will at age ninety. He died on February 1, 1702 or 1703.

"His house was on a beautiful plain near the river," wrote Samuel Deane in *History of Scituate, 1831.* "An unfailing spring, out of which eight generations of the family have been supplied, marks the spot." The Cornet Robert Stetson homestead has stayed in the family, through his son and grandson and on down to the present day. It is now known as the Stetson Shrine, and still overlooks the river the progenitor of the clan himself overlooked so many centuries ago.

The most important thing to know about your trip to Stetson Meadows is not to give up while trying to find it. Take River Street out of Norwell Center down to Stetson Shrine Lane (not Stetson Road, which will be the next road to the south). Stetson Shrine Lane ends in a cul-de-sac that sports a sign announcing the entrance to Stetson Meadows, but you're not truly there yet. There is a dirt road ahead, running along Route 3, and it's yours for the taking. Follow it as it takes a turn to the left and slopes downward. You'll get to a point where you'll think you're going to enter somebody's private driveway, and if you go straight ahead, you will. The house, the Stetson-Ford House, dates from the eighteenth century, is listed on the National Register of Historic Places and is overseen by the Norwell Historical Commission. Taking a turn around to the left, and then a quick right, a field opens that offers parking and a kiosk map of the trails available for walking.

Depending on the season, visitors will want to heavily consider the use of bug spray. The area is a haven for deer, and with deer come deer ticks. With deer ticks comes potential exposure to Lyme disease. Be careful.

There is no set way to walk the trails of Stetson Meadows, but there are highlights that should not be missed. First is the walk straight out toward the river, on the right of the open field. It leads to a small rise that overlooks the marsh. One stops and wonders if this is what the marsh looked like during Cornet Robert Stetson's time, and the answer is mixed. First, of course, Route 3 did not exist at that time, so the view to the north is changed, but beyond that, who can be sure? The Trustees of Reservations' Two Mile Reservation is across the way, another wooded parcel that overlooks the river, and the salt marsh grass is as untouched today as it was when Stetson arrived (there was a period of time in between when it was harvested heavily, as we shall see). The only thing truly missing, of course, is the occasional sailing ship being kedged downriver, as shipbuilding was well underway during the latter half of Stetson's lifetime.

One trail heads north into the woods and along the river; another leads south and turns inland, headed for a pair of towering twin pines. A hemlock grove stands out in the midst of the woods, and an ancient stone wall defines the lost boundary of neighbors from long ago. The sanctuary is not quite a bird paradise, but it does attract the typical woodland species. Listen for black-capped chickadees, tufted titmice and white-breasted nuthatches throughout the year, and in the winter watch for northern harriers flying over the marsh, hunting for voles.

For Stetson kindred, especially, though, Stetson Meadows can be a place of self-realization, the opportunity to walk the land that a distant ancestor walked and to immerse oneself in the vagaries of the past. Had Cornet Robert Stetson not liked his new home, had he been killed in King Philip's War, had he decided to stay in England and face his country's fratricidal conflict, would any of the Stetson Kindred of America be here today?

TWO MILE RESERVATION

The original Scituate stretched far beyond the borders of the town known to its current residents. Norwell, named for a paternalistic Boston businessman in 1888, was formerly called South Scituate, and once was entirely a part of the old town. Bits of Hanover, Pembroke and Hanson once shared the Scituate name. Even Marshfield lands were once considered to be within the borders of the settlement pioneered by the men of Kent. These lands, laid out by the "Two Mile" grant of 1640, though, were not originally intended to be part of the new town.

To understand the Two Mile story, one must first understand the life of Timothy Hatherly. A woolens manufacturer born in Devonshire, England, and a financier of the settlement at Plymouth, Hatherly set out to the New World in 1623 aboard the ship *Anne* to see the new colony firsthand, assess its needs and return to London to convince his fellow merchants to continue to back the people of the wilderness outpost. Hatherly learned that all was not as rosy as reports had seemed, with starvation and other hardships real worries for the Pilgrims. He stayed for two years, building a house and then watching it burn to the ground and, after being forced to relocate to Wessagussett (today's Weymouth), returning to England to work on a plan for the establishment of a Puritan community on the newly "discovered" continent.

By 1623, according to Stephen R. Valdespino in *Timothy Hatherly and the Plymouth Colony Pilgrims*, the four cliffs of Scituate had already been identified by the Pilgrims as potential building sites. And the merchant-adventurer himself was suitably impressed as well:

> There was much about the territory which Hatherly admired: the abundant saltmarshes, land-locked harbor, excellent estuary and extensive forests of hardwood trees. He also recognized the prospects for fisheries and knew the North River was a "highway into the interior," which would facilitate trade with the Indians and provide access to the vast inland stands of pine and oak. The pestilence of 1617–1619, moreover, had left the region virtually devoid of inhabitants and, as a result, Hatherly found many acres of cleared and cultivated land.

Hatherly sought a charter for the land, but had trouble securing it. Not until 1633 did he get his wish, and by then squatters had spread beyond the borders of the other

Cedar waxwings gather in large flocks in winter and assault berry-producing bushes along the North River. *Courtesy of Historical Research Associates.*

Long after the region was settled, Marshfield girls attended Camp Wy Sibo, based at Two Mile. *Courtesy of Marshfield Historical Commission.*

Some of the Camp Wy Sibo girls learned the art of kayaking. *Courtesy of Marshfield Historical Commission.*

local settlements and infringed upon the lands for which he had held grand plans. He had taken the precaution, though, of sending his nephew, Edward Foster (for whom the eponymous road and bridge leading out to First Cliff are named) to begin a settlement in the region of the cliffs with other men from Foster's hometown of Kent in 1625. Formally court-ordered parcels were laid out in 1633.

Hatherly arrived in the Massachusetts Bay Colony in 1632 to finally begin work on his dream. He became a freeman in 1633, a title necessary to have say in the governmental matters of the settlement, and moved from his temporary home in Plymouth to Scituate the following year. Almost immediately, he realized that the cliffs, North River Valley and Scituate Harbor were not all that were needed to start a community. He appealed to the General Court in January 1636 or 1637 for an expansion of Scituate lands:

> *Where Mr. Hatherly in the behalf of the Church of Scituate informed the Court that the place…is too striate for them to reside comfortably upon and that the lands adjacent are very stony and not convenient to plant upon whereby they are disabled to receive any more neighbors for their more comfortable society. It is therefore consented unto and agreed…that the said inhabitants of Scituate shall have liberty to seek out a convenient place for their residing within the colony…for their more comfortable subsistence at Scituate.*

According to Samuel Deane's *History of Scituate, 1831*, the court granted Hatherly and his fellow townsmen "all the lands between the north and south rivers, provided they make a township there," create a ferry crossing the river and passages to reach that ferry.

There was nothing better to do at Camp Wy Sibo than to join some friends on the river in a rowboat. *Courtesy of Marshfield Historical Commission.*

Before this decision could be acted upon, though, Hatherly and others received word that a 1633 request had finally come through. The Conihassett Grant, between Satuit Brook (from which Scituate gets its name, meaning "the cold brook") and the Gulph River to the north, provided Hatherly a superb opportunity. Purchasing the rights to the land from his three co-grantees, he sold the land off in parcels, keeping a quarter of it to himself and building a farm at Musquashcut Pond.

The Scituate men, though, were never able to comply with the 1636–37 grant provisos, and as such lost their opportunity to take over the bulk of the land that now composes Sea View, Marshfield Hills and North Marshfield. William Vassall, as we shall see, established a ferry across the river at about that time, separate from the Hatherly group.

But Hatherly did not give up, agitating for more land over the next few years. Finally, in 1640, the court granted a two-mile stretch of the North River to Hatherly and his associates, who empowered Hatherly to oversee its dispersion to suitable tenants. Stretching from today's Pembroke line to the corner of today's Oak Street/Union Street intersection, and reaching back one mile from the river, the Two Mile became home to Sprouts, Roses, Sylvesters and Hatches. According to Deane, "It was naturally provided with a good mill stream, and grist mills, saw mills and clothing mills were pretty early erected." Furthermore, according to Cynthia Hagar Krusell and Betty Magoun Bates in *Marshfield: A Town of Villages*, "It might have been aptly called the Mill Village or Hatchville. Almost every house was a Hatch house and every mill was a Hatch mill. The little Two Mile Brook provided water power for the mills, which supported the Hatches for over three hundred years."

William Hatch, an elder of the church in Scituate, was the first of his line in the New World, and his son Walter was the first to take advantage of the newly granted land.

Decker and Anne Hatch carried on family tradition in Two Mile that lasted more than three centuries.
Courtesy of Historical Research Associates.

William often found himself in trouble "for his loose speech concerning the government, and his manifest contempt for its authority," as stated by Harvey Hunter Pratt in *The Early Planters of Scituate*. In one instance, a witness stated for the record that Hatch referred to warrants sent for him by the governor of the Massachusetts Bay Colony as "nothing but stinking commissary warrants," comparing the "governor's summons with the process of the Scottish divorce court," according to Pratt. In another episode, the General Court had held him in "gaol" (jail) for trespassing, "for want of sureties for his good behavior."

But, when not in a state of bad humor, William Hatch served his townsmen faithfully, supporting the church, sitting on juries and leading military training of the able-bodied men of Scituate.

Walter Hatch built the house that is now known as Red House in 1647. Author Sara Messer, who grew up in the Hatch homestead, told its tale in *Red House: Being a Mostly Accurate Account of New England's Oldest Continuously Lived-In House* in 2004. Until her father bought the house in 1965, it had remained in the Hatch family for more than three centuries. Walter left two mills, a corn mill and a fulling mill, to his sons in his 1698 will; these were just the beginning of the mill invasion of the Two Mile. "There were gristmills, fulling and carding mills, sawmills, shingle mills, and boxboard mills," wrote Krusell and Bates. "These were part of the timber cutting, milling, shipbuilding complex of activities that once prospered the whole ten-mile length of the North River."

Although the neighborhood name stuck through time and the Hatches retained their hold on the land, one major change took place that forever altered Two Mile. In 1778, the Two Milers—no doubt with plenty of Hatches signing the petition—fought to be annexed to Marshfield. Scituate, presented with the idea, saw economy in it, as, apart from peninsular Humarock, Two Mile represented the only part of the community on the west side of the North River. Access to Two Mile from Scituate was dependent upon river traffic, crossing the North River Bridge several miles away to the west or taking Oakman's Ferry and heading up Union Street. The town of Scituate voted to let the annexation take place, with only two conditions: that the Two Milers give up their access to the common lands and they pay their assessed taxes. No agreement could be reached, as the salt marsh hay of the common lands was too valuable to give up. Eight years later, the same two parties met, and this time the Two Mile residents got their wish. Two Mile became a village of Marshfield in 1788.

The last mill from those progressive days stands across from the end of Pine Street and is simply known as the Hatch Mill. Constructed in stages in 1812 and 1859, the sawmill operated until 1965, handed down from father to son, like Red House. Krusell and Bates prosaically remember the last days of the operational mill:

> *Decker Hatch, the last of the millers had been running the mill for fifty-four years and his father before him for forty-nine years. The Hatches replaced the original up-and-down saw with a circular saw, and a turbine was installed in 1872. A familiar site in the early 1900s was Decker with his helpers, Elmer and Burt Fish and Peter Whynot, driving his team of horses and hauling huge pine logs down from his Pine Street wood lots. Pine slabs were taken from the mill to the Welch Company in Scituate. Tracy Magoun drove*

the sometimes frozen slabs in an open wagon across to Scituate and remembers that, by the time he arrived at Welch's, his pants would be frozen to the pine slabs. Decker was also a farmer, raising rhubarb for the Boston market in underground pit houses and hoeing his own garden until the age of ninety-eight.

Decker Hatch sold the mill in 1965 to a buyer who then resold it in 1968 to the Marshfield Historical Society. The society raised funds to restore it in the early 1970s, but fell short of its goal. In 2004, new owner Roy Kirby began a drive for the mill's restoration, creating the Hatch Mill Restoration and Preservation Group. In 2007, Marshfield Town Meeting voters approved $120,250 from Community Preservation Act money to restore the mill and create a museum. Kirby estimates that the entire project will take $1 million to complete.

Several other houses in Two Mile remain to remind visitors and residents alike of the days of the Hatches and other settlers, when the little section had its own post office, school and other buildings of communal significance.

For the nature walker, the sixty-eight acres of the Trustees of Reservations' Two Mile Reservation offers a chance to step back in time and walk the old cart paths that once led down to the edge of the North River. Perhaps the most alluring detail about the cart paths is that they are only wide enough for two people to walk shoulder to shoulder around the one-mile loop. The reservation came as a gift from Gail E. Whelan in 1993.

The views of the North River from here are more or less views of the valley and the salt marsh grasses that line either side. The water is mostly unseen but, of historical interest, Norwell's Stetson Meadows can be seen across the way. It's easy to imagine oneself as Walter Hatch, looking across the yawning expanse of the valley and wondering just what the heck Cornet Robert Stetson was up to over there.

Within the old boundary lines of the Two Mile grant, the town of Marshfield has preserved Blueberry Island, a favored resting spot for canoe and kayak enthusiasts, and the thirty-five acres of Mounce's Meadow. At the latter site, farmland formerly worked by brothers Harry and Larry Mounce—and from which Red House can be seen in the distance—bird-watchers can catch glimpses of numerous species of sparrows in fall migration and flycatchers in summer. Red-tailed hawks regularly patrol the fields looking for voles.

There is no doubt that Two Mile would have eventually been settled, had Timothy Hatherly not fought for its habitation in the second decade of European settlement of the South Shore. The question is, though, had he not done so, would the world ever have known of Decker Hatch, gentleman miller and farmer? Such are the twists and turns and "what ifs" of local history.

Nelson Memorial Forest

Each nonprofit conservation organization has its own idea of what conservation means. One allows pets on its properties, another one doesn't; one believes in taming potentially successional habitats, another doesn't. In the end, they're all saving land as open space, and that's the most important thing upon which they all can agree.

Of all the organizations saving land along the North River, whether nonprofit, municipal, federal or whatever, the New England Forestry Foundation stands out. While other organizations are doing their best to simply let nature be, the folks at the New England Forestry Foundation are actively managing the woodland of the Nelson Memorial Forest to demonstrate that we can have wood products and a healthy forest at the same time, one that offers shelter and food for all of the forms of wildlife that depend upon it.

Before there were Nelsons, there were Rogerses, and lots of them. John Rogers arrived in Scituate from Weymouth in 1644, and two of his sons, Thomas and Samuel, settled across the river at Rogers Creek (the pond at the base of Highland Road is known as Rogers Pond, and the creek flows from this spot out to the river). A third son, John Jr., also tried the Marshfield side, building a large house atop Highland Hill around 1660 and raising several Quaker children.

Practicing Quakerism at that time in the history of Massachusetts was a dangerous choice of lifestyle. Religious intolerance had reached an all-time zenith in Boston in 1658, culminating with an anti-Quaker law stating "that every Person or Persons of the accused sect of Quakers shall be apprehended[…]to close prison, there to remain without bail[…]where they shall have a trial by a special jury and being convicted to be of the Sect of Quakers, shall be banished upon the pain of death." One woman, Mary Dyer, repeatedly contested that law, was arrested several times and was finally sentenced to hang for her crimes.

One North River resident, Edward Wanton, arrived in the New World from London around 1658. Samuel Deane's *History of Scituate, 1831*, added that his mother probably came with him. We do know for a fact, at least, that he was in the city of Boston in 1659, 1660 and 1661, as he was present for some high-profile events. He served as an officer of the guard on at least one of the three occasions during which Quakers were executed in Boston during those years, and the episodes affected him profoundly.

The Nelson Memorial Forest is a haven for wildlife.

Deane wrote,

> *He became deeply sensible of the cruelty, injustice and impolicy of these measures. He was greatly moved by the firmness with which they submitted to death, and won entirely by their addresses before their execution. He returned to his house* [he was a landowner in Scituate (now Norwell) in 1661] *saying, "Alas, Mother! We have been murdering the Lord's people."*

And so began a dramatic transformation from religious persecutor to religious educator.

Disengaging himself from the city, Wanton concentrated on life on the banks of the North River, acquiring an eighty-acre farm and commencing shipbuilding, "probably, as early as 1670," according to L. Vernon Briggs's *History of Shipbuilding on North River*. He also began preaching Quakerism, corporal punishment having been outlawed by King Charles II at about the time of his conversion, winning over many prominent Scituate

White-breasted nuthatches
scurry down trees picking at
insects in the bark.

families, including some of the prestigious Cudworths. By 1678, the sect had grown so large that it necessitated the construction of a proper meetinghouse. Wanton, with others, purchased a small piece of land along the river on Belle House Neck (near Route 3A) on which to build the house of worship, but within thirty years, even that would no longer suffice. The original building, says Deane, "was sold to the Cushing family, many years after, as tradition tells, and converted to a stable."

According to Deane, writing in 1831, "Another was built, which is now standing in Pembroke, a half mile south of Barstow's bridge, in 1706." Local sawmill owner Benjamin Barker built the new house for a grand total of £111 British, and the congregation "floated" upriver to its new home. Quakers still meet at the Friends Meeting House in Pembroke, the second oldest of its kind in the country, living by the same general principles their forbears did.

The Rogerses' fears of persecution had driven one branch of the family to Vermont, where they could live in a secure Quaker community. In 1835, just before he died, Stephen Rogers of Marshfield sought a descendant to whom to pass on his two-hundred-acre farm, finding his cousin's son Moses F. Rogers and his son, the unfortunately named Stephen Rogers Rogers in Vermont. Although the land was sold out of the Rogers family in 1854, the hill on which it stood became known as Moses Rogers Hill. Henry W. Nelson bought the farm in 1872. According to Cynthia Hagar Krusell and Betty Magoun Bates in *Marshfield: A Town of Villages*, "He stocked the farm with horses, Holstein cattle, pigs and chickens. He grew crops of all sorts and maintained large greenhouses. He developed an elaborate water system that pumped water up from the brook and stored it in a large tank on the hill. He cultivated the famous Marshall strawberries and had an extensive apple orchard. The farm employed fifty full-time resident farm workers."

A packet landing on the riverbank served as a stopping place for boats bringing goods to the farmer and for others hoping to take Nelson's apples to market in Boston. The packet landing is also the site of the demise of a gundalow (a flat-bottomed, narrow-beamed boat), according to Joseph Foster Merritt in *The History of South Scituate-Norwell, Massachusetts*:

> Hatch Carver built and ran a boat from the wharf at Little's Bridge. This boat was lap streak, very serviceable, and was in use for many years being in later times owned by Freeman Damon, who lived at this landing, and carried hundreds of tons of hay. At one time it was the only boat for hire on the river and was spoken for many days in advance. It went to pieces on the meadows, having been moored back of the Nelson Farm since the '98 storm.

When Nelson passed, the land went to Margaret and Dorothea Nelson, who donated 108 acres to the New England Forestry Foundation in 1958. In later years, a gift of 22 more acres came from their heirs.

The trails of the Nelson Memorial Forest are marked for interpretation in coordination with a foldout map explaining the forestry practices taking place on the land. Certain timber lots have been harvested over the years, while others have been left to grow wild for comparative purposes. And the selection process is not as simple as one might think. Snags, or dead trees, are left to stand as future homes for woodpeckers and other cavity nesting birds, while healthy stands of trees that are competing with each other for light and water are selectively thinned. No cutting takes place within one hundred feet of the river. According to the New England Forestry Foundation, the Nelson Forest's "timber harvests have yielded over 715,000 board feet of sawlogs and 85 cords of firewood. This is enough lumber to build 50 houses and fuel to replace 150 barrels of oil." Moreover, the thinning has improved the forest to the point that the density of the stand has increased by more than 500 percent in the past fifty years.

While walking Nelson Memorial Forest, keep an eye out for the few remaining apple trees from Henry W. Nelson's farm, for scars at the bases of trees that show where logs have been dragged through the woods for final cutting and shipment and for that packet landing that once stood as an important cog in the wheel of North River commerce.

Norris Reservation

The Norris Reservation is in the heart of Norwell, and it's probably the most popular place to take a walk in town. The owner, the nonprofit Trustees of Reservations, allows leashed dogs on the property, making it a favored place for pet owners who prefer more than their typical neighborhood sojourn. It is appreciated for its natural beauty, and even for the remnants of its industrious history.

That history cannot be ignored, unless you walk most of the property blindfolded. Wide and leafy Eleanor's Path leads directly to a millpond on Second Herring Brook and the second of five dams going up the brook from the river. Chronologically, it was the first.

In 1639, house carpenter John Bryant settled in Scituate as a freeman, "ten rods east of the mill, an ancient orchard now marks the place," according to Samuel Deane in *History of Scituate, 1831*. It was his son, also a John, born in 1644, who built a sawmill on this site in 1690, and shortly thereafter a gristmill.

The importance of mills in the early days of New World settlement cannot be overestimated. Anyone with a saw or axe, gumption and a team of oxen could fell a tree and drag it to where he needed it for construction of a house or some other purpose. But to have the boards properly cut to favored widths and lengths in a short amount of time took a special skill and special equipment. Without modern sources like we have today, the power to move a saw steadily and potently enough to make boards out of timber in the New World could only be harnessed from nature. Pooling water behind a dam and releasing it to resume its natural flow at his will, a miller created that power, and as such provided a special service to the community. And where there was one mill, there were probably two or three more. Gristmills ground corn to make cornmeal, a staple of early American baking. Fulling mills cleansed and thickened wool for preparation for the making of clothes. Damming the brooks played important roles in all of these essential functions of the river communities.

According to Joseph Foster Merritt in *The History of South Scituate-Norwell, Massachusetts*, the gristmill stayed in operation through the early part of the nineteenth century, but it appears that the sawmill quickly disappeared. A new sawmill on the site appeared in 1770, only to be torn down around 1895. Over the years the ownership of the mill

The first spur trail off Eleanor's Path at Norris Reservation leads to a view of the Bryant millpond.

passed through the hands of the Turners, Proutys, Cushings, Tolmans, Merritts, Fosters, Norrises and Carsons. The last mill on the site burned on January 24, 1927. A vertical shaft from the last mill remains standing where the building once stood.

If one were to find the feeder stream leading to the Norris Reservation millpond and follow it upstream, one would come to Torrey Pond and the Torrey sawmill; Turner Pond and the Turner shingle mill; and another dam-held pond of which little is known.

Conversely, farther downstream of the Bryant Mill "is the old dam which marks the site of a saw mill which was built very early and of which little is known," says Merritt. "It was thought to have been built by one of the Bryants and that the old well and the cellar which are quite near indicate the location of his house." That site is at the head of Gordon Pond, around which a new trail system has been laid out in the beginning of the twenty-first century.

As with much of New England, few ancient trees line these paths. Walking the trails of the Norris Reservation means historically trespassing on the lands of Scituate, South Scituate and Norwell farmers of yore. The many stone walls on the property make up just a small portion of the 240,000 miles of such boundary markers in New England, and do little to explain the amount of back-wrenching physical labor that went into their creation. They lie, as geo-archaeologist Robert Thorson describes in his book *Stone By*

Norris Reservation borders the North River for quite a ways, offering stunning natural views.

Stone, at the intersection of science and history. And they're sometimes the last proof we have that settlers of European stock used lands before they became public parks. Their presence denotes the past existence of farm fields for both pasturage and croplands. The trees were cut down early and kept down.

But once the last farmer left the land and the last shipbuilder selected his final knee, successional growth occurred, leaving the lands of today's Norris Reservation with a relatively young forest of oak, pine and holly, among other species.

Early in the 1920s, Albert and Eleanor Norris began purchasing land along the river with the idea of creating a sanctuary for wildlife of all kinds. According to the Trustees of Reservations, "They eventually built a cottage, cut a trail system, opened up the shady forest to attract wildflowers and ferns, and created a haven for woodland and riverside wildlife." Eleanor donated a portion of the family land to the trustees in memory of Albert in 1970, and more in 1982. The McMullan family donated contiguous parcels in 1992, creating the McMullan Woods portion of the greater reservation, and Ralph and Elizabeth Gordon added to that in 2000. The entire reservation now measures 129 acres, with 2 miles of walking trails.

Among the most magnificent moments of walking these trails is that first minute when one realizes that he or she has reached the river. An open boathouse reaches out into

Princess pines once stood one hundred feet tall.

the water and gazes upon the bend where Rocky Reach gives way to the Rapids, and the site of the Block House Ship Yard. The historic marker is visible just downstream to the left.

The Block House yard layout illustrates the progressive thinking of the early shipbuilders, in this case the James and Tilden families, even if here, we shall see, things didn't necessarily always work out as planned. The bends in the river were utilized by many of the shipbuilders, and with good reason. Launching a ship on the river came with a significant buildup of speed on the part of the vessel. The vessel landed with a splash and its momentum carried it through the water for some way. If a shipbuilder launched a ship on a perpendicular line to the riverbank, especially on the narrower portions of the river, there was a real chance that it might simply shoot across the river and slide its way up the opposite bank. Jones River shipbuilders to the south even launched their ships sideways to try to prevent this event from occurring; if it did, they hired the local

Holly trees find their northernmost limit on the South Shore of Massachusetts.

kids to run from port to starboard repeatedly until the boat rocked its way back into the water. By building on a bend and launching diagonally from shore and directly down a channel, North River shipbuilders could give their pilots a head start downriver.

Archaeologically, there is little left of the old Block House Yard. (The name derived from the garrison house that once stood on the spot, and which underwent an attack during King Philip's War in 1676. John James, who lived nearby, died of wounds received during the attack.) But that fact is not surprising. As explained by Paul Huffington and J. Nelson Clifford in "Evolution of Shipbuilding in Southeastern Massachusetts" in *Economic Geography* in October 1939, the shipbuilders' needs were simple: "A piece of level land free from marsh, bordering on deep water, a place to pile lumber, and one or two rough sheds in which to keep plans, and perishable materials and tools completed the essentials." Like barns, shipyard structures were utilitarian, meant only to last through the jobs at hand. Also, due to the late rise of historic preservation ideals in America, which began with the demolition of John Hancock's home in Boston in the middle of the nineteenth century, there was never a movement afoot to save the historic shipyards as historic sites when they passed out of use. If the people of Massachusetts were not yet sure whether they should have saved John Hancock's house, they surely weren't ready to debate whether to save the shack in which William James kept his plans.

But the Block House Yard is remembered historically, thanks to the writing of Reverend William P. Tilden, who was born in 1811 and grew up in the yard during his father Luther's tenure there as a shipbuilder; he was quoted in L. Vernon Briggs's *History of Shipbuilding on North River*. "When I was seven or eight, my father sold the little place where I was born, and built a larger house on the bank of North River, where for some years he and his brother carried on shipbuilding together," he recalled. After going to sea with the mackerel fishery as a young boy, he slowly took up the shipbuilder's trade.

> *The daily recitations in this, my university course, needed no offset or the balance of foot-ball, base-ball, boat race, or other gymnastics, we took all that the natural way. Our broad-axes and mauls were our dumb-bells; our whip-saws and cross-cuts our vaulting bars; and deck beams, drawn up by the creaking stage on our shoulders, were our patent lifts. We worked from sun to sun in those days, often having a steaming forehood to bend after sunset, to use up the summer twilight...*
>
> *The Block-house yard was not well adapted to building. The ground was mostly springy and wet; the way to it was through a rocky pasture, with only a cart path, where deep ruts and frequent stones tried the heavy wheels, loaded with timber, and the necks of the patient oxen, which bore the swinging oak trunks, planks and knees. Then, when the timber was in the yard, there was not sufficient room for it. Beside this, when the vessel was launched, she had to run directly across the river into the mud on the other side. Souther & Cudworth's Yard, a half mile up the river, and Foster's, above that, were far better yards; more spacious, and with a finer chance for a glorious launch up or down a long reach. Still there were many vessels built at this yard. But the Block-house, though not a No. 1 ship-yard, was a glorious place for us boys.*

Tilden recalled swimming parties with friends, skating in winter and knowing it was time to start looking for eels when spring peepers began their seasonal chorus.

Leaving the boathouse and the days of the Block House Yard, the McMullan Trail leads to the River Loop Trail, sticking close by the water's edge. At a scenic vista at the southernmost bow of the trail, it's possible to look out across the river and marsh to the town of Marshfield's Cornhill Woodlands. In late fall and winter, northern harriers may be seen above the marsh searching for food, while flocks of wild turkeys and small groups of white-tailed deer move throughout the woods. If you look closely, you'll see that the Norrises' plan has come to fruition. Ferns, princess pines (diminutive trees that historically stood one hundred feet tall) and young white pines soak in the sunshine beneath their towering oak, pine and beech brethren. A clearing near the end of the loop boasts a large, round millstone that once did work so important to the people of South Scituate.

Crossing the
North River

As important as it was to establish industries on the river, to build ships, to harvest salt hay, to fish and to transport locally grown apples to distant markets, it was equally as important to find the most advantageous spots at which to cross the river. The trick was to do so without disrupting the flow of ships, salt hay, fish and apples. Excepting for the Route 53 and Route 3 crossing sites, all of the bridge sites downriver were laid out prior to 1660.

The construction of bridges impacted shipbuilding on the river in a unique way. Far from creating an obstruction to getting ships downriver, they instead served as a trade highway for goods moving back and forth from Boston to Plymouth, with the shipbuilding towns benefiting from being innocent waypoints between the two growing communities.

While North River shipbuilders relied little on outside markets—at first—for their primary raw materials, they did need a steady influx of secondary, manufactured materials that were being fabricated elsewhere. Rope rigging, for instance, could be obtained from Boston and, after 1824, from the Plymouth Cordage Company. Canvas came mostly from St. Petersburg, Russia, and, after the local bog iron ore was depleted, Sweden provided the product of choice for Plymouth County forges tasked with fashioning chains and anchors.

Thus, with the need for imported goods high and, ironically, the fact that a rare few of the ships built on the North River could ever return to it because of its lack of depth, intercepting that Boston to Plymouth mercantile traffic became a necessity.

Luddam's Ford

Crossing the river did not mean necessarily doing so on a permanent structure connecting the two sides. Crossings came in three styles: fords, ferries and bridges.

Luddam's Ford in Hanover and Pembroke is not on the North River, but instead on the Indian Head River, one of the two sources that converge downstream at "the crotch" to create the main river. But its importance to the history and lore of the North River cannot be understated.

Just off the well-beaten path, this plaque on the old North River Bridge tells the story of days gone by.

Governor John Winthrop of the new Massachusetts Bay Colony, on a return visit from Plymouth, noted in his diary in September 1632,

> *About five in the morning the Governor, and his company came out of Plimouth. The governor of Plimoth* [William Bradford] *with the Pastor and Elder, &c, bringing them nearly one-half mile out of town in the dark. Lieut. Holmes with two others and the Governor's mare came along with them to the great swamp, about ten miles, when they came to the great river, they were carried over by one Luddam, their guide, as they had been when they came, the stream being very strong and up to their crotch, so the Governor called the passage Luddam's Ford.*

As noted by L. Vernon Briggs in *History of Shipbuilding on North River*, "No other name has ever been given to this locality, and no more appropriate name could be given." The only name missing is James, oh he of strong back, the first name of the man who carried the governor across the river.

The general area of Luddam's Ford became increasingly important to the life of the river as time advanced. Fisheries and agriculture preceded the 1704 construction of an anchor forge by Thomas Bardin, who extruded iron ore from the local bogs to create his

Union Bridge once drew up to allow vessels to pass by, and also catered to more horses than cars. *Courtesy of Historical Research Associates.*

masterworks. During his time, Briggs estimates, the first bridge crossing the river came into being. Later, after the site passed into the hands of the Curtis family, the federal government came calling for anchors to be made for the new frigate USS *Constitution*. Military contracts would always be welcome, and helped keep the industry alive during the Civil War, at a time when shipbuilding on the North River was trickling to a halt. The forge site gave way to the 1873 Clapp family rubber mill, which grew from three employees to approximately one hundred in just over a decade, and encompassed both sides of the Indian Head River. The current West Elm Street Bridge, running to the northeast of the mill site, was completed in 1894.

The area surrounding Luddam's Ford today is a nature walker's paradise. Luddam Ford Park, maintained by the Hanover Conservation Commission off Elm Street, offers more than twenty-two acres of open space, including a stretch of retired railroad bed that runs alongside the river. Across the river, on the Pembroke side, the Indian Head River fish ladder evokes memories of the long-gone days when shad, alewives and even salmon spawned in the river. Deane tells of the extinction of alewives in the North River by 1831, due mostly to the construction of milldams. Briggs mentions an attempt to bring back salmon in the latter half of the nineteenth century, as "a few years ago the river was stocked with several millions of Oregon salmon, but they have all disappeared."

Farther upstream from the fish ladder on the Pembroke side sits the Tucker Preserve, owned by the Wildlands Trust, more than seventy-five acres of open space with trails abutting the river. An Eagle Scout project in 2001–02 provided benches for walkers

The view from the Norwell Canoe Launch certainly highlights the beauty of life along the river.

needing a moment's rest along the paths and a small bridge crossing the stream that marks the boundary between the preserve and the town's parcel.

James Luddam would be so proud.

North River Bridge

The single most important crossing of the river during its heyday as a shipbuilding center stood, in various iterations, and indeed stands today, on Washington Street, on the Hanover-Pembroke line.

Twenty-three-year-old Englishman William Barstow left his homeland for America on the *Truelove* on September 20, 1635, with his younger brother George, settling at Dedham the following year, being a signer at the town's incorporation. In 1638, he married Ann Hubbard, and some time after 1640 removed to Scituate, where he appears as a freeman in 1649.

His ancient place of habitation, though, today is in Hanover, "about one hundred rods north-west of Hanover corners, on the east side of the Plymouth road," according to Samuel Deane's *History of Scituate, 1831*. Like Cornet Robert Stetson in the land

For many years, before it became the smallest state park in Massachusetts, Chief Justice William Cushing's gravesite lay hidden in the woods. Cushing's grew up along the banks of the North River. *Courtesy of Scituate Historical Society.*

that would eventually become Norwell (it became South Scituate officially in 1849 and Norwell in 1888), Barstow can be called his community's first citizen. Hanover separated from Scituate in 1727.

Barstow's North River legacy revolves mostly around his construction and maintenance of a bridge crossing the river approximately fifty feet southwest of the current North River Bridge. In 1656, he accepted twelve pounds sterling to "make a good and sufficient bridge for horse and foot over the North River, a little above the Third Herring Brooke, at a place called 'Stoney Reache,'" according to Massachusetts Bay Colony Records. For that twelve pounds he was also charged with laying out and clearing a "way towards the bay as far as the Hugh's cross brooke." Ever the entrepreneur, Barstow kept a tavern nearby as well. He also stood to receive twenty more pounds from the colony for keeping the bridge in good repair between 1662 and 1682, but he died in 1668.

In 1682, the Colony Court upgraded the local infrastructure by ordering the construction of a cart bridge over the same passage that until then had only afforded access to pedestrian and equestrian traffic. The court charged three communities for its construction, collecting ten pounds from Scituate and five each from Marshfield and Duxbury. This crossing, still known as Barstow's Bridge long after its namesake's passing, remained in operation into the 1820s.

The disappearance of the tollhouse at Little's Bridge marked the end of an era for many South Shore residents. *Courtesy of Historical Research Associates.*

Crossing Little's Bridge heading south meant a journey into Marshfield, and straight up a steep hill that taxed many early automobiles engines. *Courtesy of Historical Research Associates.*

Barstow's Bridge became an important link between Boston and Plymouth, allowing mail and other goods to be transported along the "Plymouth road." Historians have repeated the fact in numerous publications and, indeed, on the historical marker that overlooks the northeasterly flow of the river from the North River Bridge, that in 1800 that stretch of river supported an inordinate number of shipyards in comparison with the rest of the waterway. Paul Huffington and J. Nelson Clifford wrote in "Evolution of Shipbuilding in Southeastern Massachusetts" in *Economic Geography* in 1939,

> *Of the total of thirty yards on the river, a concentration of twelve firms was located on the downstream side of the old North River Bridge, over which the Boston to Plymouth road passed. The reason for the premium put upon this area was that supplies coming from Boston traveled over this road by wagons. As no ships could navigate the river, these yards received supplies most easily, roads to the other sites being little more than rough trails.*

Thanks partially to the bridge and road and partially to a positive confluence of economic factors—a great demand for fish for trade and consumption, low tariffs for American vessels engaging in domestic and foreign trade, the lack of a good land-based transportation system and the seemingly inexhaustible supply of oak and pine in the lands surrounding the river valley—shipbuilding on the North River hit its peak in the first decade of the nineteenth century.

In 1829, the Plymouth County Commissioners decided the time had come for a third bridge to be built at the crossing. L. Vernon Briggs, in *History of Shipbuilding on North River*, stated, "The middle pier of this bridge was taken entirely from one rock" from a wall on a local field. By that time, North River shipbuilding had begun a long, slow decline, but the bridge had not been built with that industry in mind. According to Briggs, "The road over Barstow's Bridge became the old Turnpike Road, and thousands of times have the old stages, loaded with passengers and freight, dashed down the hill, over the bridge and up the other side, the horses leaping almost out of their traces as they sped up to the Quaker Meeting-house Shoals."

That bridge gave way to the fourth and current structure, built in 1904. That arch was completed just in time to be the scene of a mock battle between Massachusetts militiamen and "invading" forces from other states. The *Rockland Standard* reported on July 16, 1909, that that town "may be visited by the state troops of Massachusetts, Rhode Island, Connecticut and other states during the week of August 14 to 21, during the war game which is to be tried out under the command of Gen. Leonard Wood, Commander of the Department of the East" and a hero of the Spanish-American War.

The plan called for "enemy" troops to try to invade Massachusetts and fight their way to Boston, while everyday life rumbled along around the conflict. "The towns hereabouts may be right in the thick of the war game," said the *Standard*, "and in order to prepare themselves the selectmen of the various towns have been notified by the authorities that the troops may operate hereabouts." The state's adjutant general promised that officials would survey the battlefields after the maneuvers had ended and would "estimate any possible damages to fences, walls, etc., and pay cash as soon as an agreement is reached."

Heading north was much easier, except for the fact that the driver had to control the speed built up heading down from Marshfield Hills. *Courtesy of Historical Research Associates.*

Sea View was aptly named; from the neighborhood one could see the Sea Street Bridge, the Hotel Humarock (on the right) and, in 1909, the wreck of the schooner *Helena*, to the left. *Courtesy of Historical Research Associates.*

The combined forces of New York, Connecticut, Rhode Island, New Jersey and the District of Columbia struck with mock fury into the defensive line set up by the Massachusetts boys from Plymouth to Rhode Island. Outstanding tactical maneuvering by the invaders set them free on a straight course toward Boston, but the Massachusetts force caught them from behind, engaging them in a pitched battle at Hanover Four Corners and over the North River Bridge. Hanover historian Barbara Barker picks up the story, from her "Focus on History" column:

> One of the largest encampments was located in the Sylvester fields, near the present Cardinal Cushing School. Many of the men were farmers, factory workers, shop keepers, and the like and were unused to the rugged terrain and work. Some were called "tenderfoots." Some got lost as they charged the enemy through the swampy areas, and didn't find their way out for two days. Many such exhausted men were carried out on stretchers. Many begged food from the country folk, because their camp was miles away. Some wells in Hanover went dry, because of the demand for water…
>
> The men trampled fields like cattle as they charged the enemy. The heaviest cannon fire occurred on the last day, when the two forces met on a nearby site. The detonation of the cannons, which was set off on Broadway, broke dishes from shelves in neighboring kitchens and broke every pane of glass in Herman Sturtevant's house (427 Broadway).

When the invaders failed to take the bridge, they fell back, giving the field, and the "war," to the boys from Massachusetts.

Other than that, it's been a pretty quiet place.

The Bridges that Weren't

At least two suggested crossings never came to be, at almost the same place. Samuel Deane reported,

> In 1785, a subscription was raised to build a bridge across the North River near John Stetson's (the ancient Wanton place). The Town chose a Committee to consult with the subscribers, and to learn what kind of bridge was proposed, and how to be kept in repair. The Town then voted their consent, on condition that a sufficient draw be kept. The project then failed. It was revived again in 1827; but is not yet accomplished.

And it never was.

A century later, Joseph Foster Merritt wrote in *Anecdotes of the North River and South Shore* in 1928, "About fifty years ago there was a project on foot to build a bridge across near what was then the David Barnes Ford place in South Scituate, now owned by George Morton, but nothing ever came of it. This would have made a short cut from 'Church Hill' to the 'Two Mile.'" The blame, according to Joseph C. Hagar in *Marshfield: The Autobiography of a Pilgrim Town*, fell squarely on the shoulders of the residents of the

Marshfield side, when "the people of North Marshfield failed to get action on a petition for a bridge over the river at the mouth of the Two Mile brook." Oddly, Merritt blamed the people of his own hometown. "The Town voted to oppose the petition and the plan fell through," he stated in *The History of South Scituate-Norwell, Massachusetts.*

Oakman's Ferry and Union Bridge

After Luddam's Ford had made its mark on North River history and before William Barstow built his first bridge, Elisha Bisbee took on the challenge of maintaining a ferry service between Marshfield and Scituate (now Norwell) in 1644 at the site of today's Union Bridge. His successor, Captain Tobias Oakman, left his name to the operation, which became known throughout history as Oakman's Ferry. Because of its position relative to other ferries farther downstream at the site of today's Route 3A and at today's Sea Street Bridge, going over to Humarock, it was also known as the Upper Ferry. The last ferryman to run the Oakman route back and forth was the coincidentally named John Tolman. Although the days of the local ferryman had ended, his mark has been left on the river. According to Merritt, "The old ferry boat that did service here was hauled up in a ditch on the Thomas meadow and for many years parts of it could be seen sticking out of the mud."

In 1799, Scituate proposed to build a bridge jointly across the span with Marshfield, but Marshfield refused to pay its share of the cost (Scituate had raised $370 for the purpose), and a private corporation stepped in to accomplish the project. Union Bridge opened in 1801. Hatch Tilden collected tolls there for more than four decades, and the bridge became a free crossing point in 1850. The Union Bridge was replaced in 1899, 1917 and in 1958, and is now again in need of serious repair.

As Americans moved into the vacation and recreation era and away from sunup 'til sundown toil, they began seeking out people with common interests in the art of spending free time frivolously. Not long after the last ship was built on the river, and while gundalows still pushed quietly up and down its course with mounds of salt marsh hay, new, smaller types of boats became prevalent on the North River. Local boys who could afford them and summer visitors who had more money than they had ideas for spending it purchased small pleasure boats of all kinds—rowboats, canoes and small sailboats—and turned the river from an exclusive place of work to one of seasonal leisure time enjoyment.

On the Norwell side of the river, just downstream of the Union Bridge, the North River Boat Club opened its doors on June 18, 1894, "with speaking, boat racing, tubraces and fireworks and dancing in the evening," according to Merritt. "It was very pleasant on a Sunday afternoon to watch the boats manoeuvre, and the evening assemblies, with the building and town landing decorated with Japanese lanterns and red fire and White's orchestra playing the popular airs of those days, were looked forward to by the young folks for miles around."

The Union Bridge still connects Norwell's Bridge Street and Marshfield's Union Street today. On the Marshfield side of the river, just upstream of the bridge, is a Marshfield conservation parcel used as a canoe launch. From roughly 1701 to 1848 it served as the Brooks-Tilden shipyard, from whence the *Abigail*, the *Debby*, the *Erie*, the *Three Friends* and others slid down the ways and into maritime history.

Doggett's Ferry and Little's Bridge

Perhaps the bridge most associated with the North River for people crossing the river in modern times is the Route 3A Bridge, historically known as Little's Bridge. This is obviously not the most heavily traveled bridge in modern times, nor is it the most historic. But other than the tucked away Union Bridge, it offers the most tangible proof that one is actually crossing a river, in the form of a dramatic backdrop of an expansive salt marsh, moored pleasure boats and a river flowing out to sea.

William Vassall was the first to settle the land on the Scituate side of where today's Route 3A crosses the North River. Granted two hundred acres of land in 1634–35 "on condition that he keepe a ferry against his farme," Vassall maintained the New Harbour Ferry from his home on Belle House Neck (land later owned by the family of Chief Justice Cushing; his mansion stood on the site of the current Cushing homestead site on Neal Gate Street), a territory he called West Newland. Vassall, who always seemed to be embroiled in some form of political turmoil, experimented with oyster farming on the banks of the river, apparently quite unsuccessfully, before removing to Barbados, where he died in 1655.

The Doggett family took control of the ferry and ran it for nearly a century and a half before the construction of the first bridge at the crossing that by then had adopted their name. The first Doggett to inhabit the area, Thomas, built a farm in 1659 on the Marshfield side of the river, downstream near the mouth.

In 1825, Little's Bridge, named for the family of Captain George Little, who owned land up the hill from the crossing on the Marshfield side, stood for the first time. Constructed by a private firm, like the Union Bridge, Little's Bridge came with a toll that had to be paid by every person wishing to cross it. In this case, it cost one cent to cross on foot, eight cents for a one-horse carriage and ten cents for a two-horse carriage. One perhaps apocryphal tale states that the clergymen from Scituate and Marshfield, when crossing the bridge, would meet in the middle, dismount their horses and cross the center of the bridge on foot, then trade horses and save themselves all but the one-penny charge apiece.

L. Vernon Briggs told of a particular ship captain who had no patience for an undrawn bridge at the site:

> *Timothy Williamson used to run a packet sloop between Boston and North River. He was a great gunner, and, being usually the only man on board his small craft, he would begin firing his "flint-lock" some time before reaching the drawbridge, in order to have it opened for him. Those living in the region of Little's Bridge remember hearing the "bang," "bang," "bang," and they always knew it was Tim Williamson coming up the river.*

He once shot and killed a shark near the bridge, with no mean struggle against the beast. Williamson's hot temper and his propensity for playing with guns eventually got the better of him, as he accidentally shot himself in 1846, doing permanent injury.

Five years later, on the night of April 16, 1851, tides got so high that the bridge had to be closed from both sides. Some time after midnight, Minot's Lighthouse toppled into the sea, killing the two keepers assigned to "keep the lights burning" that night, Joseph Wilson and Joseph Antoine. The storm has forever since carried the lighthouse's name.

From 1851 to 1864, the family of Edwin Curtis collected the fares. When Curtis left for the Civil War, his wife Augusta and daughters Evelyn and Augusta ran the operation, even after hearing that Sergeant Edwin had been killed on June 19, 1864, of wounds received while fighting with the Fifty-eighth Massachusetts Volunteer Infantry at the battle of Petersburg, Virginia. On March 20, 1865, the bridge became a free crossing, which was happy news to the ears of many travelers.

Lysander Salmon Richards wrote in *History of Marshfield, Mass.* in 1901,

> The author remembers, when a young man, living in his native town of Quincy, Mass., of driving to Marshfield occasionally, and being obliged to stop and draw his wallet to pay toll at a house close to the bridge on the Marshfield side, now, in 1900, owned by the town and let as a residence.
>
> During his drive from Quincy to Marshfield, he was stopped on turnpikes and bridges for toll two or three times, which was certainly a great nuisance, and the law passed by the state freeing all bridges and turnpikes was certainly a righteous act.

The tollhouse of which Richards spoke was moved from its riverside site in 1926, to the lament of Joseph Merritt, who wrote,

> With the removal of the Old Toll House at Little's Bridge, Marshfield, another landmark of the olden times has disappeared. The ordinary motorist on his way to the Cape speeding up to make the hill just over the river, or returning, in a hurry to reach home after a day spent there, would hardly notice the little house just by the road which the widening of the highway in the interest of that same motorist has condemned to go the way of all things that stand in the way of progress.

The bridge on the "shore road" to Plymouth got replaced in 1933, and then again in 2002 with today's 2,650-foot-long structure, a luxurious and quick crossing of which William Vassall, even with his fertile mind, never dreamed.

On June 10, 2006, the State of Massachusetts renamed the bridge for twenty-six-year-old Sergeant Michael Jason Kelley, a 1997 graduate of Scituate High School who lost his life fighting for his country in Afghanistan with the Massachusetts National Guard.

The Railroad Bridge

Downriver of Little's Bridge and crossing the New Harbour Marshes and Fourth Cliff Bay, the Duxbury and Cohasset Railroad chugged its way into history at a most amazingly ironic moment. In 1871, shipbuilders had reached the absolute end of their days on the North River. That year, when the *Helen M. Foster* rolled down the ways from the Chittenden Yard, the shipbuilding industry on the North River died. Several factors led to the ignominious end. The call for increasingly large vessels of drafts that the river could not handle; increased costs in getting large vessels to sea from North River yards; the removal of a fishing bounty that once supported local fishermen; the exhaustion of white oak trees along the river; the transfer of financial capital from maritime interests to railroads and other investments out west; new trade agreements with Great Britain; and the expansion of the freight-carrying railroads themselves all contributed to the end of shipbuilding on the North River.

In 1871, the Duxbury and Cohasset Railroad crossed the river for the first time, symbolically stamping out the last vestiges of a once thriving industry. An extension off the Braintree-to-Cohasset South Shore Railroad line, the Duxbury and Cohasset line brought visitors to the beaches of Marshfield and Duxbury and to the heart of Kingston until 1939, disrupted only during the Portland Gale of 1898. The railroad bed—heightened after that Portland Gale—remains mostly intact today across the river, minus its drawbridge, best visible from Damon's Point Road, which was formerly a part of the corridor itself.

White's Ferry/Sea Street Bridge

The first two crossings mandated over the North River came near the ocean. Just a few years after William Vassall organized the New Harbour Ferry, the General Court in 1638 ordered the arrangement and maintenance of a second ferry, downriver close to the mouth of the rivers. The new ferry, run by Jonathan Brewster of Duxbury, operated from an active packet landing on the property of Peregrine White, the first child born to the Pilgrims in the New World. As such, it earned the name White's Ferry. In 1645, ferryman Ralph Chapman found himself in a financial crunch and petitioned the General Court to set him free from his duties, "as it would bring him to extreme poverty." The court responded by allowing his freedom, "except on special occasions, as bringing over the magistrates who dwell there."

White's Ferry—the place, not the boat—also served as the fitting out station for ships built on the river. When they were launched, North River ships had neither masts nor sails. Pilots worked them downriver with kedge anchors until they reached White's, where their masts would be stepped and they would be rigged for passage to the sea. The only steamboat ever built on the North River, the *Mattakeesset*, was built here at White's in 1839.

The later nineteenth-century initiation of the South Shore towns as summer destinations for the rich and famous sparked interest in Humarock and its sandy beach.

A new hotel on the peninsula, erected around 1890, called for direct access from the mainland by a way other than the barrier beach road that then ran between Third and Fourth Cliffs, so the first Sea Street Bridge was built in 1892. The current bridge, built in 1952, was renamed the Captain Frederick Stanley Bridge in a ceremony in 1998 marking the centennial anniversary of the Portland Gale of 1898. Captain Stanley led the crew at the Fourth Cliff Life-saving Station from the 1880s to the 1910s. In 2007, the Sea Street Bridge closed for demolition and replacement.

The Julian Street Bridge, built in 1942, was reconstructed in 2007 and reopened in the late fall of that year.

Modern-day Crossings

While the romanticism of later bridge building efforts is clearly miniscule when compared to the early days of fords, ferries and stone bridges, the fact is that twentieth-century crossings have made significant impacts on the vistas and health of the North River.

Route 139 begins in Stoughton and ends at an intersection with Route 14 in Duxbury, crossing the North River just southwest of the old North River Bridge on Washington Street. Governor James Michael Curley called for the widening of the road during his tenure in office, 1935–37, and the federal government allotted $450,000 for the Depression-era project.

Construction began on Route 3 South—or the Pilgrims Highway, as Governor Foster Furcolo so named it in 1960—as far back as 1948. Americans were clear of World War II and were feeling the need to roam. Well-stocked by the nation's growing automobile manufacturing interests, and later influenced by President Dwight D. Eisenhower's creation of the Interstate Highway System, they demanded roads on which to use their new Ford Thunderbirds, Oldsmobile 88s, Packard Clippers and Studebaker Commanders. A superhighway connecting Boston to Plymouth and Cape Cod became a necessity and, as with the construction of the North River Bridges centuries earlier, the North River towns stood to be affected by a major roadway passing through their borders.

The four-lane section of Route 3 that crosses the river was the last section of that roadway to be completed, stretching from exit 13 in Hanover to exit 10 in Duxbury. Route 3 South opened in full in 1963, cutting across the salt marsh between exits 12 and 13 near an area known as Bald Hills.

The North River Wildlife Sanctuary

Mass Audubon's North River Wildlife Sanctuary attempts to embody the entire North River experience in one site. There's tangible cultural history derivable from the magnificent old manse that now serves as Mass Audubon's South Shore Sanctuaries' regional office building and the comparatively quaint cottage and stoic barn tucked into the trees. There is a sublime natural experience to be had by walking the Woodland Loop Trail or the River Loop, with its offshoot Red Maple Swamp Trail. The agrarian history of the area can be read in stone walls along the field's edges and even in the trees that stand quietly on the property, keeping the secrets of the past to themselves. Purple martins loop around in the sky in summer, as do tree swallows, while red-tailed hawks soar overhead. And from the river view boardwalk and platform, installed by legendary local birder and former Marshfield conservation agent Warren Harrington in the early 1980s, the vast final turn of the river is visible as its waters spill out past Fourth Cliff to the sea.

As with many old residences in Plymouth County, the current sanctuary's history can be traced back through several centuries. And as with many such places, the lot of land that is called the sanctuary today is a byproduct of those few centuries of real estate wheeling and dealing, of deaths and wills and ultimately of a gift to a nonprofit organization.

Land along or even near the banks of a river provided several advantages for an enterprising type of person in the early years of New England settlement. Rushing water meant mill-turning power, and it meant swift transport for products grown or made on the river. One such settler, a gentleman named Amos Rogers, received a land grant in 1702 that included what became known as the appropriately named Riverside Farm site. His son, also an Amos, married into the Wales family in 1757, and together he and his wife Rachel raised their first three children—Rachel, Persis and Atherton Wales Rogers—to adulthood, losing their next five in infancy.

Rachel Rogers, at twenty-two, married Captain George Little during the American Revolution, just a year before he set sail as first officer on the new brig *Protector* to harass the British Royal Navy. (That adventure landed the captain in British hands, ticketed for a London prison, but he bribed a sentry and escaped to France. But I digress.) Captain

The Killam-Rodgers estate, which became the North River Wildlife Sanctuary office, was once surrounded by an army of evergreen bushes. *Courtesy of Mass Audubon.*

Little offered his father-in-law £110 for the precious land, including eighty acres of the Clift family farm. Little and his bride passed their land on to their oldest son, Edward Preble Little, who brought the whole thing back around again by marrying another Rogers (Edy, of a Pembroke family). He later married a second time, to Beulah Brown of Lynn in 1824.

At about that time, America's concept of the best usage of waterfront property began to change. With America beginning the Industrial Revolution–inspired shift from a primarily agrarian economy to one fueled by the fires of large-scale factories, those people who owned the factories started to dabble in the notion of spending time away from their workspace, an idea completely foreign to America's farming families. A society that was once known to communally toil from sunrise to sunset had begun to split into haves and have-nots, factory owners and factory workers.

Escaping work also meant fleeing from the very same creations that had both lined their pockets and given them the freedom to roam: the factories. And more than just escaping the structures themselves, what the big businessmen of the day sought relief from were the sounds, the smells and the sights of urbanized areas: smokestacks belching smoke and ash, machines grinding away noisily and the stark utilitarian imagery of

This side view of the North River Wildlife Sanctuary has been entirely swallowed up by trees today. *Courtesy of Mass Audubon.*

progress at work. Instead, they sought ocean or mountain views, fresh air, sunshine and, eventually, porches from which to view them all, another invention of the middle of the nineteenth century. The country gradually moved away from needing either a spiritual or physical regeneration as an excuse to stop working, to simply having enough money to not have to worry about such things in the first place.

And so it was with the land of today's North River Wildlife Sanctuary. The land passed through the hands of several owners before it landed in the hands of Enos M. Stoddard of the Boston Ice Company. When he died in 1905, the estate, by then 180 acres large, fell to his son, Charles Dudley Stoddard. In that year, Charles Stoddard married Nova Scotian widow Arabella Cann Killam. Her two daughters who moved into the house with them, Elizabeth and Constance, would eventually will the entire estate to Mass Audubon. Killam's son Izaak stayed in Canada, but would impact the estate in future years.

Believe it or not, a decade later Elizabeth, known as Betty, married another Rodgers, Ralph of Marshfield; the only difference between him and the rest of the Rogerses who had lived on the land was the additional letter in his surname. At that time, to accommodate the newlyweds, the family had what is now the caretakers' cottage moved from the river's edge to its current position. Route 3A once ran through what is now the front yard of the cottage, but it was moved to make room for the building. In this house Betty and Ralph raised a son, Walton Killam Rodgers.

Meanwhile, in Canada, Izaak Walton Killam was making himself a fortune and secretly becoming one of the richest men the country had ever known. By 1919, he had purchased controlling interest in Royal Securities, financing paper, pulp and hydroelectric

Although the methods have changed, Mass Audubon workers still cut the hay in the field of the North River Wildlife Sanctuary like the many farmers who came before them. *Courtesy of Historical Research Associates.*

projects across the country and even in Latin America. In 1923, by then married, he spread some of his wealth to his mother and sisters, paying for the remodeling of the houses on the Marshfield estate. His legacy lives on both there and in the Killam Trusts (funding sources for five Canadian universities), at a hospital and library named for him in his native land and in two biographies: *Canada's Mystery Man of High Finance: The Story of Izaak Walton Killam and his Glittering Wife Dorothy* and *A Very Private Person: The Story of Izaak Walton Killam and his Wife Dorthy*.

Ralph Rodgers died in a flu epidemic in 1926, and Charles Stoddard passed away in 1933. When Arabella died in 1937, she left the whole estate to her three children, which, in actuality, meant the two sisters, as Izaak was financially set for life.

Tragedy struck for the family two days after Thanksgiving in 1944. On November 25 of that year, a day on which the aircraft carriers USS *Essex*, USS *Intrepid*, USS *Cabot* and USS *Hancock* were all struck by Japanese kamikaze planes off Luzon in the Philippines, Lieutenant, junior grade, Walton Killam Rodgers, United States Naval Reserve, was pronounced as missing in action in the Pacific. Betty, hoping he would come back, remained in the cottage for the next few years, but eventually gave up hope and, heartbroken, moved back into the main building with her sister.

Izaak Walton Killam passed away in 1955, but his sisters survived into the 1970s. Betty left this world in 1975, and Constance in 1977. Their wills provided Mass Audubon with the house and grounds, and some funds for an endowment for the operation of a wildlife sanctuary on the property. Several neighbors of the sanctuary today still remember "the ladies" and cherish their memories. After a couple of years of legal red tape (one persistent rumor claims that Boston Bruins hockey great Bobby Orr lived in the house for a short time), Mass Audubon took control of the land.

Changes came quickly. Caretaker Brian May and his family moved into the smaller half of the main building in 1980, and soon thereafter the old barn that then stood across from the main house on Summer Street was moved to its current spot off the main driveway into the sanctuary's parking area. The half-circle parking area on Summer Street in front of the main door is now gone, evidenced by the patchwork masonry in two sections of the stone wall out front. Two years later, a young and energetic director named David Clapp arrived from his previous position as director of the Moose Hill Wildlife Sanctuary in Sharon to begin educational programming, advocacy and community relations for the new sanctuary. He stayed for more than two decades, moving into the cottage and raising his children there. When he retired in December 2005, he opened the door for an interesting twist. His position was eventually taken by Sue MacCallum, education coordinator at Drumlin Farm Wildlife Sanctuary in Lincoln and the wife of Brian May. Brian, Sue and their three kids had just moved out of the caretakers' apartment when the director's job opened up. Sue, who had moved into her new home down the street, had commuted to work in Lincoln from the North River Wildlife Sanctuary for more than two decades; in June 2006, the sanctuary became her daily destination, rather than her daily departure point.

The North River Wildlife Sanctuary office today is a beehive of activity throughout the year, with children's nature camps in summer, a weekly Friday morning birding program more than two decades old, a gift shop open year-round and education programming running for students of all ages. The staff oversees a total of six wildlife sanctuaries in Mass Audubon's South Shore Sanctuaries region: North River, Daniel Webster and Tilden Farm in Marshfield; North Hill Marsh in Duxbury; Stump Brook in Halifax; and Assonet Cedar Swamp in Lakeville.

Before even stepping onto the trails at the North River Wildlife Sanctuary, one's attention is drawn to a tall, canopied tree in front of the house, and with good reason. Camperdown elms are rare on the South Shore (others can be found in front of the Hull Public Library and in Jackson Square in Weymouth, among other places). The tree is a cultivar with a canopied top grafted onto the upright stalk of a Dutch elm (and as such, is susceptible to Dutch elm disease). All Camperdown elms in the world came from one tree in Scotland, on the estate of the Earl of Camperdown in Dundee, Scotland. The estate's head gardener found a mutant plant growing on the grounds and performed the first graft some time between 1835 and 1840. Victorians loved the curiosity of it, and those in America who could afford it imported it. The Camperdown elm in front of the North River Sanctuary's office building produces abundant shade on hot summer days, and was used by education coordinator Ellyn Einhorn for years as "the gathering tree" for kids' programs. The Stoddard family probably planted the tree during their tenure as owners, some time during the latter half of the nineteenth century.

Stepping off the well-kept lawn and onto the Woodland Loop Trail, one immediately discovers an old foundation, that of the home of Calvin Ewell. One wonders how such

The view from the cathedral landing window of the North River Wildlife Sanctuary office looks out upon purple martins, red-tailed hawks and the North River.

1. Part of the fun of debating which view of the North River is the best one is trying them all out.

2. The beauty of Stetson Meadows makes even a Carolina wren want to sing.

3. The Pembroke Quakers still use separate men's and women's entrances when entering their meetinghouse.

4. Several members of the Rogers family that owned today's Nelson Memorial Forest practiced Quakerism. Quakers continue to follow their faith today at the Pembroke Friends Meeting House at the intersection of Routes 53 and 139.

5. Once known as the Rapids, this stretch of river was once populated with sailing ships headed to sea. Now it's as quiet as a ghost town and is enjoyed by thousands who walk the trails of Norris Reservation throughout the year.

6. Remnants of the ancient Bryant mill site remain at the Norris Reservation in Norwell. The last mill on the site burned down in 1927.

7. Tree swallows gather at the mouth of the North River and in other coastal locations to fatten up before heading south for the winter.

8. The Norris Reservation boathouse is a South Shore landmark.

9. Shipbuilders laid out their yards on river bends, like this one, where the Block House Yard once sent its ships off to sea.

10. One of three fire control stations at Fourth Cliff, this tower stands alongside a modern cottage available to America's servicemen and -women for their family vacations.

11. The remnants of the abutments of Barstow's Bridge remain today.

12. The modern Washington Street Bridge steers traffic away from the old bridge and from tangible history of the North River.

13. Today's Union Bridge is in need of repair.

14. The view from the Marshfield Canoe Launch, just across the bridge from Norwell, also provides a great view.

15. Today's caretakers' cottage at Mass Audubon's North River Wildlife Sanctuary has a sad history, being the home of a Marshfield man lost in action in World War II.

16. The North River Wildlife Sanctuary feeders attract birds that like to feed on other birds, like this Cooper's hawk.

17. The sanctuary also attracts ruby-throated hummingbirds in summer.

18. Rare wildflowers, like this whorled pogonia, secretly grow on the North River Wildlife Sanctuary.

19. The construction of the battery at Fourth Cliff included the ingenious disguise of one of the fire control stations as a summer cottage.

20. After the Portland Gale, those folks living on Third Cliff could no longer walk directly to Fourth Cliff.

21. Without protective measures, the piping plover may be extinct within a few decades.

22. Piping plover eggs are well camouflaged, which protects them from predators but makes them difficult to discern by the human eye.

23. The Pembroke Canoe Launch at dawn can be one of the most serene places on the North River.

24. As with so many other places along the North River, the view from the base of Riverside Circle can be sublime.

25. The old Duxbury and Cohasset Railroad bed still runs mostly intact across the New Harbour Marshes, as viewed from Damon's Point in Marshfield.

26. The marshes along the rivers are excellent staging areas for monarch butterflies in migration.

27. A visit to Damon's Point will be a surprise to those who enjoy birds. One resident at the end of the street believes strongly in providing shelter for the little creatures.

a small house could have satisfied human needs, but then, life was much simpler before electricity. The trail continues eastward past a spur trail that leads to the maintenance area of the sanctuary, and finally onto the intersection that puts the "loop" in "loop trail."

Oak, white pine and American beech trees dominate the landscape, some growing to enormous size. Occasional mixed flocks of birds flitter through the woods, with black-capped chickadees and white-breasted nuthatches chattering away as they hop from tree to tree in search of food. Red-bellied and downy woodpeckers are known to breed here, as are great horned owls and eastern phoebes. In April, water can run down the trails like a stream; in September, mushrooms of numerous types sprout from the ground. In December, tracks in the snow prove the existence of white-tailed deer on the property, although from time to time they simply walk along the driveway anyway, and such proof is not needed. Cover boards set out for campers along the trail's edge hide red-backed salamanders. Fifteen species of ferns line the trail, as do princess pines. Rare whorled pogonias grow in two secret, protected locations, safe from orchid collectors.

The Woodland Loop Trail, winding past an understory of American holly trees, highbush blueberry and sweet pepperbush, ultimately descends into a grove of witch hazel trees, the latest blooming tree in New England. A visit here in October or November is well worth braving the colder temperatures, as the explosion of yellow flowers in the midst of an otherwise drab, winterized forest is a sight to see. Ancient beliefs held that if a man snuck up on a witch hazel tree on midsummer's eve, reached down between his legs and pulled off a switch, he could then use that switch as a dowsing rod to find not water, but gold.

Another spur trail shoots down to a boardwalk that overlooks the Hannah Eames Brook, named for an early resident. (Hannah Trouant married Jonathan Eames in 1682, and they had a daughter named Hannah Eames in 1684; Hannah Decrow married Amos Eames in 1769, and they had a daughter named Hannah Eames. Take your pick.) The brook runs past American hornbeam or sinewy "musclewood" trees, a regularly occurring tree along the waterways that feed into the North River.

Across Summer Street, the River Loop Trail begins, sloping gently downhill toward the river basin, although that slope doesn't necessarily seem so gentle on the return trip. At the top of the field an anomalous clump of trees stands watch over the field, the place where the barn used to be. It stands as an excellent example of what would happen to the rest of the field if it was left to regenerate to forest. Fisher tracks have been seen in the snow here, and in the spring American woodcocks use it as a hiding place after finishing off their dramatic courtship displays in early April. The field itself is a study in modern open space management. Today, as during the past few centuries, the field is maintained as a hayfield, or cultural grassland. Cultural grasslands, fields created for farming by mankind by cutting away forest, are rapidly disappearing in the Northeast. As such, birds that use such habitats, like bobolinks and eastern meadowlarks, are threatened with extirpation as the fields disappear. Mass Audubon's current ecological management plan calls for the field to be kept open, or to keep alive a habitat that is not native to Massachusetts (it was originally forest) to keep birds that are not native to the state (they moved in from the west when the fields were opened by the early farmers) here.

Elsewhere in the field, tree swallows dart back and forth feeding on insects, prompted to live on the property by the maintenance of a series of nest boxes. Two tall poles in the middle of the field hold rows of hollow plastic gourds, the preferred nesting places of rare purple martins. In recent years, Marshfield has been home to one-third of the purple martins nesting in Massachusetts. Late spring storms that have coincided with their annual migration, though, have caused drops in the numbers of nesting pairs both at the North River and at Daniel Webster Wildlife Sanctuaries. Preferring to feed on high-flying insects, the birds are susceptible to starving during periods of extended rain.

Purple martins once nested in natural cavities in trees, but Native Americans figured out that by hanging gourds around their villages they could utilize the birds' choice of diet to their advantage. The birds nested in the gourds, zapped bugs and over generations forgot about natural cavities altogether. Today, they will only live in man-made housing.

While the main trail heads on a beeline directly for the river's edge, a quick diversionary route cutting through an ancient stone wall curls through a red maple swamp to the east. Evidence here suggests that some of the trees in the area gave up their best wood for the shipbuilding industry. By watching for multiple shoots coming from a single base, one can see where the original cut was made and guess the age of the tree.

The loop trail reaches a second intersection at the base of the hill and descends onto a boardwalk that in springtime especially helps keep the walkers' feet dry. Skunk cabbage sprouts here in the spring, as does jack-in-the-pulpit under the thick canopy. A right-hand turn off the trail brings sunlight and a short walk out onto a platform for a view of the river. In winter, Bonaparte's gulls fly over the water in search of food, and harbor seals gather on the floats across the river to partake of the sun's warming rays. In summer, great egrets and great blue herons slowly stalk the marsh, spearing small fish and frogs. To the east, Fourth Cliff is clearly discernible. To the northeast, one can spot the retired railroad bed of the old Duxbury-Cohasset line and Wills' Island. To the west, the Route 3A Bridge dominates the view.

The North River Wildlife Sanctuary provides four centuries of history as well as a glimpse at the ever-dynamic face of nature in the Northeast.

DRIFTWAY CONSERVATION PARK

O kay, it's not technically on the North River, but there are few places that evoke more poetry about the river's colonial existence than the stretch of First Herring Brook that runs from James Landing to the main waterway. For visitors today, it offers an accessible glance, even by automobile, of what the river once was, with views across the salt marshes to the old military tower on Fourth Cliff. But even at that, the modern-day interpreter of the river's past must take caution.

William Gould Vinal, perhaps the greatest nature educator the South Shore has ever known, studied the history of the North River in myriad ways. In his booklet *Salt Haying in the North River Valley (1648–1898)*, he discusses the economic impact of salt haying on local communities; his personal memories of days growing up a "Mt. Blue boy" in South Scituate (he was born there before it became Norwell) wherein there were many adventurous outings "down meadow" with his father; and even the history of local children using the outdoors as a venue for learning about life, something he lamented was vanishing when he wrote in the 1950s. If he could see where we are today, he might once and for all concede defeat on the topic.

Vinal's work reminds us that the North River salt marshes of yesteryear, specifically pre-1898, were much more extensive than they are today. "No farmer had a more beautiful view; no Pilgrim a more peaceful scene," he wrote of 1890s trips to his father's meadow. "The great salt marshes; the cobalt bay with white caps; the Third and Fourth Cliffs with an unbreached barrier connecting them; unmarred Coleman Hill, a recessional moraine; and wooded Wills's Island, our destination."

Salt marsh haying came as necessity for early settlers. As Scituate historian and schoolteacher Bob Corbett Sr. has quipped, had America been settled in reverse, from California to the East, racing wagon trains would have reached New England, looked at all the rocks coming out of the ground, thrown up a fence and declared the region the country's first National Park. But, unfortunately for those first settlers, the land they chose to till did have those unending rocky-floored forests, with the freeze-thaw cycle bringing up new stones every year. They had to cut down the trees to create the fields and remove the rocks (actions from which most of our stone walls have sprung) to plant the seeds to make their English hay grow. This process was inherently time-consuming,

HERRING RIVER, (GREENBUSH), SCITUATE, MASS.

The Driftway is not along the North River, but off a major tributary to it, the Herring River. *Courtesy of Scituate Historical Society.*

in terms of seasons. They needed hay in the meantime, for roof thatch, for "banking their houses," or insulation, as Vinal explains, and for feed for cattle and horses. Stated matter-of-factly, "Without free thatch for rooftops and black grass for hungry cattle, existence might have been dubious."

The salt marshes met all of the above-mentioned needs, and as such they became highly coveted. They demanded no tilling and no planting, just harvesting. After two hundred years of harvesting, "there was no soil deterioration," said Vinal. "The property is passed on from generation to generation in as good condition as it is received." As such, he adds, "Is it any wonder then that salt meadows were mentioned in nearly every official document in the Plymouth County right up to the Storm of '98?"

Many of those official documents had to do with land ownership. The Two Mile grant, for instance, had mostly to do with access to salt marshes. To this day the topography of the river reflects property disputes and agreements from ancient times. Joseph Foster Merritt picks up the story in *History of South Scituate-Norwell, Massachusetts*: "After a time transfers began to be made and divisions of estates brought it about that in many instances, people who owned the meadows lived some distance from them. They were for the most part surveyed and the rights of way many of them had over adjoining property were in many cases bones of contention and litigation and are even to this day [1938]."

This image, taken by Lennie Arnold and now in the collection of the Scituate Historical Society, shows a ditch dug as a boundary during the hay gathering days of the North River's past. *Courtesy of Scituate Historical Society.*

The Boston Sand and Gravel Company took away the heights of Colman's Hill, seen here. For comparison, the current Scituate Maritime Museum is at left. *Courtesy of Scituate Historical Society.*

In all, the Boston Sand and Gravel Company removed millions of cubic feet of sand from Scituate. *Courtesy of Scituate Historical Society.*

Those disputes spilled over onto the marshes themselves. "Anyone traveling over the salt marshes to and from Little's Bridge can observe salt marsh ditches," noted Vinal. "Why were they made? Which tools—shovel, spade, pitch fork, or saw, were used? This is the $64.00 question." It took the memory of an eighty-nine-year-old, Luke Fitts, thinking back to stories his grandfather had told him for Vinal to find out. "The line ditches marked boundaries," he concluded after an oral history with Fitts. "These were necessary to prevent the indiscriminate cutting of hay. The side ditches came in at right angles to help drainage. The meadow lines were marked off into rectangles because this was an old English custom." A lasting side benefit of the digging of the ditches is the mosquito control they provide, the draining off of stagnant pools of water in which the pesky insects breed.

The physical act of gathering salt hay took two distinct forms, defined by the method of hauling the crop off the chosen meadow. First, there was reliable land-based transport. The salt marsh farmer would sharpen his scythe on a whetstone and get right to work, swinging back and forth, mowing down a swath through his meadow. His crew, consisting many times of young boys of his own or from the neighborhood, bunched the hay with a pitchfork and then slid two "hay poles" (eight to ten feet, cut from white cedars or hemlocks) under the load and carried it upland, where a cart would be waiting. The smell of freshly mown salt hay was as distinct as a freshly mowed lawn today.

If a farmer felt lucky, or that his particular rectangle of salt marsh had unusually firm footing, he shod his horse with specially made marsh shoes and led it out into the marsh, which cut down on the marsh to upland travel for his poling team. The horse's wooden salt marsh shoes slipped over the hooves and provided a wider base on which to stand than the hoof normally offered, much like a snowshoe does for humans, notes Vinal. While they are now out of use, it is possible to see marsh shoes as artifacts at the Scituate Historical Society's Cudworth House Barn on First Parish Road.

In those areas where land transportation was unfeasible, or where a disputed right of way cut a salt marsh hay gatherer off from his crop, transportation by water became a necessity. Gundalows—long, flat-bottomed boats, sometimes square-ended, sometimes with ship-like bows—slid silently up and down the river with crews of five or more (on oars, fending poles and sweeps, usually with a couple of extra boys to help "rake scatters"), the signature work craft of the industry in the river valley. Some men liked them big, like the Henderson brothers of Norwell, who uniquely carried their horse, cart, twenty-foot loading planks and cutting tools with them on their gundalow, and John and Frank Turner, whose gundalow was so large the locals nicknamed it "Jumbo" for P.T. Barnum's elephant. Others, though, preferred them small enough to navigate the creeks and "guzzles" off the river. L. Vernon Briggs tells in *History of Shipbuilding on North River* of the construction of three gundalows at Union Bridge by Cummings Litchfield, which he named *Eureka*, *Red Rover* and *Sea Boy*. Merritt adds in *History of South Scituate-Norwell, Massachusetts* that *Sea Boy* rested on the landing at Union Bridge for years before succumbing to the elements and going to pieces. These boats used several landings that connected to roads to bring their cargo ashore, like at Union Bridge.

The biggest, most venerated foe of the gundalow arrived in 1870. "The Duxbury and Cohasset Railroad Bridge was built quite close to the water and it was always a thorn in the flesh of the old river men," said Merritt in *History of South Scituate-Norwell, Massachusetts*, "as a loaded boat could not pass under at high tide." A gundalow owner need not have owned a section of salt marsh. Instead, he could hire himself and his boat out to marsh owners as a river-based freight carrying line.

In later years, after English hay had been established on local farmland, salt haying took place only after the rest of the crops back home had been started. It served as an important

Some of the sand went by train, much of it by water. *Courtesy of Scituate Historical Society.*

substitute during winter days when the regular stock was running out. If harvested in summer, it was carted at night, to avoid mosquitoes and biting greenhead flies. "Black grass," or salt marsh rush, grew above the high tide line and provided the best feed. "Marsh hay," or salt meadow cordgrass, and "salt thatch" plucked from the intertidal zone admirably performed on roofs and between walls. After the first crop had been taken, marsh owners returned for "rowens," or the second cut, of nutritious timothy and heather.

There was a social side to salt marsh haying as well. Challenges issued exhorted men with scythes to compete against horse-drawn cutters. Wrote Vinal, "The man with the horse broke a part of the machine and had to take it to the blacksmith. He still won." Salt marsh hay gatherers became ornithological experts in the local shorebird species, knew the best hunting spots for waterfowl each fall and understood the gastronomic value of many of the other plants that grew on the salt marsh.

Local oral tradition tells us today that the Portland Gale, with its inrush of salt water that killed off much of the salt marsh grasses, also killed the industry, but Vinal states that "the time was coming when hay of any kind could not be given away. Salt hay would have passed out of the picture whether nature sent a violent northeaster or not." The steady decline of the use of cattle created a concurrent decline in the need for salt hay. "That is one of the most significant changes in the last fifty years; hay most valuable crop, to hay, a fire hazard, even the hay fields going back to the forest," said Vinal. The industry died like any other; when demand ran out, suppliers moved on to other, more lucrative fields, in this case literally.

Though the "gundalow days," as Merritt called them, are over, their memory lingers in works such as his and Vinal's. Vinal wrote,

We no longer pole hay, especially the salty kind. And I doubt if we seek the intimations to be drawn from such rough tasks as haying or squinting river-ward to see a solitary

The end for the sand and gravel
company came by fire in 1963.
Courtesy of Scituate Historical Society.

*sandpiper. Some of our most enduring literature has arisen from just such simple scenes.
It is true that science is electrons and atomic bombs, but nature or American literature
is also going to the salt meadows in late summer, the gathering of shore birds in flocks,
and the appreciation of sweet grass and sea lavender. It is well, I am certain, to store
up such memories in the days of youth for the poetry that will be in the heart in the
days to come.*

The Driftway Conservation Area also represents another considerable change from
the days of the men of Kent. When they arrived in the area in the 1630s, the land
along what would become today's Driftway was dominated by an enormous, nearly
vertical-faced wall of sand. Joseph Colman, a shoemaker by trade, settled in Scituate
early enough, possibly by 1635, to be one of its first constables, and his oldest son, also
a Joseph Colman, received the sandy hill upon his father's death. Joseph Jr., a Quaker,
moved to Connecticut in 1690, leaving behind that unstable mound that came to be
known as "Colman's Hill." A landing nearby accommodated loads of salt hay coming
ashore.

The hill lorded over the developing community along the Driftway and "at the
green bush" (the neighborhood today known as Greenbush) for two centuries before
a man of entrepreneurial spirit decided to roll the dice and invest in the future of the

area. Capitalizing on the arrival of the train to the region and the establishment of the Duxbury-Cohasset line in 1870, designed to lure city dwellers to the shore, Boston businessman George H. Eaton built a hotel atop the western end of Colman's Hill. This establishment was complete with more than one hundred stairs leading directly to the eminence and a sweeping road curving its way to the top for carriages and "barges," horse-drawn carriers that transported people and baggage from train stations to lodging. The hotel opened in 1871, but by 1872 was doomed. The Great Boston Fire of that year bankrupted many of its backers, including Eaton himself, who left for the American West. According to Merritt in *Anecdotes of the North River and South Shore,*

> *The hotel was rented and was opened for several seasons, but it was never very successful. The inconvenience of reaching it outweighed its advantages and it was finally closed as many seasons as it was open. For several seasons the young people of Greenbush held dances there and those occasions are remembered with great pleasure as it was very pleasant and cool on a hot summer night.*

By the end of the nineteenth century, the hotel proved to be a complete bust, referred to locally as "Eaton's Folly."

In 1914, a new venture moved into town, one that finally altered the landscape in ways unimaginable to the men of Kent. The Boston Sand and Gravel Company arrived and began cutting away at Colman's Hill, by that time also known as Hotel Hill (the hotel soon burned). Sand was moved by train and by barge, headed for Boston, by way of the old salt marsh hay landing and others built specifically for the new purpose. Much of the sand went to create the foundation for Logan Airport. The statistics are staggering. Between 1922 and 1931, the company removed 6,148,000 tons of sand and gravel, or 2,000 tons per day for six days a week. From 1947 to 1963, it moved 200,000 tons per year. Most of Colman's Hill vanished as hills that once stretched forty feet into the air disappeared entirely. The company sometimes dug down to below sea level. A network of roads moved and evolved with the operation, sliding along the Driftway to meet the needs of the latest excavation. In all, 14,000,000 tons of sand disappeared from the topography.

The landscape has changed further still. On July 18, 1963, the buildings and equipment of the Boston Sand and Gravel Company caught fire in a conflagration so grand that many Scituate residents still use it as a guidepost marking a significant moment in their lives. Today, ask anyone who was living in town in 1963 where they were when the Boston Sand and Gravel fire broke out, and they can give you exact details. Today, the new Massachusetts Bay Transit Authority Greenbush commuter rail station and the town's recycling and transfer centers stand where George H. Eaton once thought he'd find gold.

The Driftway Conservation Park offers short walks that in summer allow one to look barely above the tops of the salt marsh grasses. There are also picnic tables and a recently contested boat launch. The remains of the old docks and the foundation of old buildings can be seen throughout the 450 acres of the park, reminiscent of just one use of the land since the men of Kent arrived in the seventeenth century.

FOURTH CLIFF

They weren't settled in order, but somehow Scituate's first three numbered cliffs were all thickly populated well before what is probably the most famous cliff of all, the fourth. When one examines the topography of the town of Scituate, it's easy to see why. Scituate's natural harbor, or at least what became the harbor, sits north of First Cliff (a report by the federal government after dredging the harbor channel in the 1800s told of cedar stumps stretching across the mouth between Cedar Point and First Cliff, hinting that the harbor may have at one time been a pond that gave way to the sea). First and Second Cliffs shield the landward approach to them across Edward Foster Road and the marshland it traverses. Third Cliff offers the same convenience with access via the Driftway. But Fourth Cliff, even before the 1898 breakthrough of the beach that reached from it to Third Cliff, has always stood alone.

The fact was that when Scituate was settled, that beach connected the two cliffs, albeit in a tenuous way, and the rest of the land now known as Humarock was a southward-reaching peninsula. It made no sense for Marshfield to claim it, for there was no landward approach to it from their town, with the North and South Rivers flowing out from between the southern end of the peninsula and Rexhame. The irony today is, of course, that for Scituate residents to get to Humarock by land they have no choice but to go through Marshfield. So, with no access from the Marshfield side, and limited access from the Scituate side, Fourth Cliff became a tough sell for farmers looking to till the Scituate soil.

Apparently, though, the Tilden family was up to the task, as generations lived on the cliff over the course of centuries. Nathaniel Tilden, who arrived on the *Anne* in 1623, built his house on Kent Street in Scituate and soon became one of the wealthiest men around. "He had left a comfortable, not to say pretentious home in England for a rude dwelling here," said Harvey Hunter Pratt in *The Early Planters of Scituate*, "that he might obtain the greater spiritual solace of an unhampered devotional." Among his holdings were extensive parcels of salt marsh inside "New Harbour," the basin inside Fourth Cliff prior to the 1898 creation of the "New Inlet." The Tildens and their descendants obviously fought for the protection of their shore-side land from erosion, even though it was so removed from the heart of the community, as Samuel Deane states, that "the

Fourth Cliff, in the distance, lies at the mouth of the North River. In the middle of this image, the open field of today's North River Wildlife Sanctuary breaks up the otherwise dominately forested landscape. *Courtesy of Mass Audubon.*

beaches eastward from Third Cliff to the river's mouth, have been defended from waste, by repeated acts of the Town, forbidding the removing of stones, &c."

The last Tilden homestead on Fourth Cliff was built in 1828, but the family would not be alone for much longer. The Humane Society of the Commonwealth of Massachusetts erected a hut of refuge at Fourth Cliff in 1857, across from White's Ferry, leaving it in the care of John Tilden, who also had control of the society's lifeboat there as late as 1869. These small tools were all that stood between many mariners and their deaths from shipwreck, and the system of placing lifeboats along the coast at key spots was later copied by the U.S. Life-Saving Service, which eventually became the basis for today's Coast Guard search and rescue stations.

The Fourth Cliff Life-Saving Station stood from 1879 to 1919. *Courtesy of Scituate Historical Society.*

Around that time, too, came an early boardinghouse. By the middle of the nineteenth century, as discussed in the chapter on the North River Wildlife Sanctuary, Americans began vacationing more and more. As described by Joseph Foster Merritt in *Anecdotes of North River and South Shore*, looking from the Driftway toward the cliff "a lone two story building and an old barn were for a long time the only structures to be seen. This was the Fourth Cliff House, one of the first summer boarding houses on the South Shore. Long before the days when summer people were coming in any number to Scituate and Marshfield a few families who had discovered the place and liked the quiet were in the habit of spending their vacations there." William Merritt and family arrived to run the Fourth Cliff House in 1879, catering heavily to shorebird hunters each spring and fall.

That same year, the United States Life-Saving Service built its Fourth Cliff Life-Saving Station at the southern end of the hill. For the next nineteen years, surfmen working under Keeper John Smith and then Keeper Fred Stanley patrolled the sands from the southern end of Humarock to Scituate Harbor, treading nightly across the linking beach between the cliffs until November 27, 1898, when the Portland Gale took their passage away.

Fred Stanley lived the life of a typical lad of his era, educated in the Boston schools until twelve and then sailing off to sea as a cabin boy. "He followed the sea until he was

Wreck of the Schooner Helena, Jan. 31, 1909, Scituate, Mass.

The Fourth Cliff crew, led by Captain Frederick Stanley, saved the crew of the schooner *Helena* in 1909. *Courtesy of Scituate Historical Society.*

twenty-three years of age," according to the *Biographical Review for Plymouth County, 1897,* "circumnavigating the globe more than once, doubling Cape Horn and the Cape of Good Hope, and visiting the principal maritime countries of the globe." Retiring from the sea, he took up fishing and Irish mossing in Scituate and joined the Life-Saving Service in January 1880, taking over as keeper just nine months later. He and his wife Julia, whom he married in 1868, built a house at Third Cliff. His commute to work became much longer after the Portland Gale.

Even prior to the opening of the Cape Cod Canal in 1914, coastwise traffic along the western shore of Massachusetts Bay could be heavy, with goods being moved amongst Boston and Plymouth and the other, smaller ports in between. Northeast storms could push vessels not even contemplating visiting these ports down onto the beaches below the cliffs, at which time Stanley and his men went into action with lifeboat, surfboat or the breeches buoy apparatus. They became renowned for their rescues of the crews of the *Agnes R. Bacon,* the *Minnie Rowan,* the *Helena* and more. In 1893, the *Annual Report of the Life-Saving Service* stated that emergency measures had to be made, as "the sea was making dangerous inroads upon the station, and it was deemed advisable to move the station to a secure position, which was done."

The turn of the century brought several changes to Fourth Cliff. The Portland Gale disconnected the cliff from Scituate proper in 1898, and the Fourth Cliff House burned down in 1902. The U.S. Army Corps of Engineers arrived in 1910 to survey the North River with intentions of digging a canal to connect it to the Taunton River, but not a single shovelful of dirt was ever removed. By that time, the sands of Humarock to the south were beginning to sing with the sounds of summer frolickers, with the large Hotel Humarock just across the Sea Street Bridge boasting electricity in every room and a telephone in the lobby. Daniel Webster Clark arrived and began building cottage-style houses with an eye toward luring wealthy summer visitors to the beach in season, but still, the northern end of the peninsula remained quiet.

(Humarock probably derived its name as a corruption of its historic names, "Shore Hummocks" and "Hummock Beach," found on nineteenth-century maps. Scituate town records from 1732 list it as Humock Flatt or Hummock Flats. All of this research can be found on the internet at www.humarock.net, the community's website.)

In 1919, the Fourth Cliff Life-Saving Station burned down. By then, the face of coastal lifesaving had changed. Motorized lifeboats had replaced pulling boats as early as 1907, and communications technology had improved as well. Although the practice of men walking patrols at night with kerosene lamps (and later, flashlights) would continue into the 1930s, for the most part, it was a dying art. And by 1919, the Coast Guard (the Life-Saving Service had merged with the Revenue Cutter Service in 1915 to become the Coast Guard) had moved away from building stations that forced their crews to launch directly into the surf, and toward protected launching spots for motorized boats. The Coast Guard remained active at the North Scituate station on Surfside Road before moving into its new quarters on First Cliff in the 1930s. The Fourth Cliff station was never rebuilt, and the land upon which the station sat still remains empty today, at the eastern end of River Road.

With the Coast Guard gone, the navy moved in. Captain Linwood S. Howeth, U.S. Navy, stated in his *History of Communications-Electronics in the United States Navy* that,

> *In early 1918 the Chief of Naval Operations, concerned with the delays of transports by weather conditions, directed his Planning Committee to study the subject and endeavor to eliminate these delays. The Committee recommended the establishment of direction-finder stations in groups of three around the approaches to the harbors of Boston, New York and Charleston, and the entrances to the Delaware River and Chesapeake Bay…This was approved, and in June 1918 the sites for these stations were selected.*

And thus in 1921 was born radio compass station (later radio direction finder station) NX5 Fourth Cliff. The navy purchased a little more than two and a half acres from the Tapley family of Danvers, owners of land on the cliff that reached back through at least one generation, stretching from the river to the sea. The direction finding system called for three stations working together to help guide convoys in and out of the harbors through fog and other inclement weather, to hopefully help them speed past potential U-boat attacks. "One station of each group would operate as the master or controlling station and control a transmitter at a distant station by landline," wrote Howeth. "The two 'slave' stations would telegraph their bearing to the master, where the plotting would be done and fixes or bearings transmitted to the convoy commander." Fourth Cliff worked in conjunction with radio direction finder stations at Deer Island in Boston

Harbor, and Gloucester and later Thacher's Island on the North Shore. In 1924, the navy constructed a barracks building at Fourth Cliff.

As development continued on Humarock, houses crept closer to Fourth Cliff. The cliff's next tenant would use this fact to its advantage.

In the 1930s, with America's participation in the global conflict of World War II looming, the United States military began focusing on the country's shorelines and its potential vulnerabilities. The Boston Harbor area had been fortified since the 1600s, but many of the facilities had not been updated since the first decade of the twentieth century. A new standardization plan called for their enhancement and for the construction of four new batteries of coastal artillery, including one at Fourth Cliff. "The harbor defense modernization program proposed a uniquely camouflaged gun battery and three fire control stations at Fourth Cliff to extend the southern defenses of Boston Harbor," wrote Gerald W. Butler in *The Guns of Boston Harbor*. "When complete, the gun battery and other military structures at Fourth Cliff—coded *Location Number 114*—would appear to be a continuation of the shoreline summer cottages and resorts."

Survey work took place in 1941 and the army began buying up all fifty-seven acres of the cliff, allowing the navy to remain in place on its two-and-a-half-acre site as "Project Silver Sands" rolled around it. In September 1942, work began on Battery 208. A year later, a pair of six-inch guns mounted on M-4 barbette carriages and "equipped with experimental electronic tracking and gun-laying systems," according to Butler, sat on either side of the earth-covered magazine, which hid the battery's power plant and plotting room beneath it. Atop the magazine sat an imitation cottage, the basement of which served as one of three spotting stations. A second fire control tower, to the south, was camouflaged to look like a house, while a third, to the north, was not. Small houses, used mostly as barracks, popped up along the western shore of the cliff, complete with pastel paint jobs and garden plantings.

Within two years, the site outlived its usefulness. World War II ended, and with the advent of the jet engine, coastal defense was moving from the land to the air. It was now the U.S. Air Force's turn.

The newest branch of the American military, having broken off from the army in 1947, took control of Fourth Cliff in February 1948, assigning it to the Cambridge Field Station as a research annex. Three barracks on the northernmost reach of the peninsula, which was rapidly eroding away, were sold to private bidders and moved off the reservation that September. The site changed names to the Fourth Cliff Electronics Research Annex in 1955.

During the Cold War, antenna towers were built onsite for "both radar surveillance and experiments in tropospheric radio propagation (scatter communications) and air-to-ground communications," according to Butler. "The experiments had final application to Distant Early Warning (DEW) and Ballistic Missile Early Warning (BMEW) defenses." In 1956, the site's most significant contribution to the history of scientific discovery was made.

According to scientists Jules Aarons and William R. Barron in the August 4, 1956 edition of *Nature*, "An effect of the solar flare and cosmic ray increase of February 23 reported by several observers was recorded on the atmospheric noise study apparatus located at the U.S. Air Force Cambridge Research Center site at Fourth Cliff, in Scituate, Mass." Solar flares are violent explosions in the atmosphere of the sun that produce ultraviolet radiation and X-rays that can interfere with radio communication on Earth. The results are almost instantaneous; one particularly large flare on January 20, 2005, had effects on our planet in just fifteen minutes, in the form of the most powerful proton storm ever recorded. Solar flares have been studied since 1859.

Cosmic rays, on the other hand, are tiny, mostly hydrogen-based particles that travel toward our atmosphere at nearly the speed of light from two sources: the sun and outer space. Our atmosphere acts as a barrier, intercepting most of them and breaking them into smaller, secondary particles before they can get to the Earth's surface. What Aarons and Barron were excited about was that the disturbance recorded—the sudden increase in radiant energy being absorbed by the Earth's atmosphere—happened at night. Thus, for the first time, a SID (sudden ionospheric disturbance), identifiable by unexpected enhancement of radio signals, was traced to cosmic rays and not solar flares.

Perhaps fittingly, the final stop for Fourth Cliff to this point in its history is relaxation. After a few short years in "maintenance" and "caretaker" status, the Fourth Cliff site became a recreation site for military personnel in 1964. By the mid-1970s the antennae came down, some of the base's buildings were restored, new cottages were built and recreational vehicle pads were laid out.

The future for Fourth Cliff, though, continues to be as fragile as the glacial till that forms it. In 2001, the U.S. Air Force commissioned a study of the area by ocean and coastal consultants. The study concluded that two main factors, wave action at the base of the cliff and storm water runoff from its top, were to blame for the continuing erosion on the site—the same erosion the Tilden family complained of in the 1600s. Several alternatives were suggested, from sand replenishment on the beach (a sacrificial dune) to stabilization of the cliff through planting vegetation to an "armor stone toe protection." The goal of the project is for the cliff to survive a one-hundred-year storm event.

Ironically, the study also showed that the sediment eroding from the cliff is moving to the north and northwest, meaning that it is feeding Third Cliff and flowing into the outlet of the rivers. In other words, it is helping to close the mouth of the North River.

Mother Nature moves in mysterious ways. And sometimes she moves in perfect circles.

THE NORTH RIVER AND THE PORTLAND GALE

I t's already beyond living memory, and continues to fade from the handed-down oral tradition, but there can be no denying the awesome impact the Portland Gale of November 26–28, 1898, had on the South Shore of Boston.

The numbers are overwhelming. At least 350 ships received some form of damage during the storm from New Jersey to Nova Scotia, either being battered to pieces on shore by the winds and waves, run aground or sunk entirely. Approximately five hundred people lost their lives to the storm, including almost two hundred aboard the steamer *Portland* alone, for which the storm was named.

Lifesavers from New Jersey to Maine rescued 120 more people from sure death during the three days of the storm, which was actually the convergence of two weather systems over New England that combined to create a super storm, and its aftereffects. In Hull, Keeper Joshua James and the men of United States Life-Saving Service Station Point Allerton saved 20 men from four ships over thirty-six hours. In Marshfield, the crew at the Brant Rock station had to seek refuge in the stone chapel across the street when the ocean surged through their boat room doors. Water breaching Duxbury Beach kept the patrolmen of the Gurnet Life-Saving Station in Plymouth from making their appointed rounds.

As the storm approached Scituate and Marshfield on Saturday, November 26, one of the lifesavers (known as surfmen) from the Fourth Cliff Life-Saving Station, Richard Wherity, felt it was his duty to warn the hunters who annually found their gunning huts each November, when migrating ducks made their return to the area, of the impending meteorological mayhem. But the temptation to linger in the salt marshes was strong for the hunters. Of particular interest to local sportsmen at that time of the year were the three species of scoter ducks—black, surf and white-winged—which they colloquially collectively called "coots," not to be confused with the American coot, a different bird entirely.

Some gunners, as they were called, looking for coots rowed out along the beach before sunrise in small dories and anchored themselves in long lines perpendicular to the shore. The birds flew in predictable aerial pathways from the north, parallel to the coast, and could be drawn in with decoys. When flights passed overhead in loose formations

The goal of coot gunning was more quantity than quality of birds killed. *Courtesy of Scituate Historical Society.*

consisting of all three types of scoters and possibly a few common eiders and oldsquaws (recently renamed "long-tailed ducks"), numerous guns popped at once and gunners began arguing over who got what before the birds even hit the water. A good day's hunting could net fifteen to twenty birds.

But there was no guarantee that a wounded bird would easily be retrieved. Scoters are excellent divers and have been known to feed at depths up to forty feet below the surface. Once in the water, they will literally swim for their lives. Some birds would rather commit suicide by drowning, clinging onto firmly rooted grasses with their bills, than be caught by gunners.

Some gunners, like the Clapp brothers of Scituate's Greenbush section and the five young Norwell men in the Henderson party on November 26, preferred to do their reconnoitering from small wooden shanties they'd located in the salt marshes. One of the Clapps, Everett, even had his own trained flock of Canada geese to use as live decoys to bring the birds in close enough to shoot.

Once back to the center of town with their catches, gunners had the option of keeping their prizes for their families or selling them to local taverns or hotels, which vied for the distinction of having "the best coot stews in town." Ironically, according to many recipes of the day, even "the best coot stew" was among the most unpalatable meals in town. For example, a *Field & Stream* recipe from 1924 said to "take the goodly coot and nail it firmly to a hardwood board. Put the board in the sun for about a week.

At the end of that time, carefully remove the coot from the board, throw away the coot and cook the board." Other recipes say to boil a coot with potatoes and carrots for a few hours, throw in an old shoe, remove the coot and eat the shoe. Edward Howe Forbush stated in his *Birds of Massachusetts and Other New England States* that "the younger birds have been found quite palatable, if skinned and dressed at once," but "if allowed to hang long with the viscera unremoved, they become vile. I recall a case where a lady cooked such a bird, thereby driving everybody out of the house. She had to throw away both bird and kettle."

Coots taste so bad in a stew because they're bottom-feeding birds, which means they tend to be very oily. When they are cooked in a stew, they become saturated in those oils.

But the Clapp boys—Everett, William and Richard—and the Henderson party—Fred and Bert Henderson, Albert Tilden, George Ford and George Webster—weren't worried at all about debating the pros and cons of the taste of a stewed coot on November 26, 1898. Thanksgiving had just come and gone, and the holiday weekend was still young. There was plenty of time for innocent revelry in the magnificence of the season on the river, and certainly plenty of hunting to be done.

George Woodman, a Trouant's Island resident, visited the Henderson shanty behind Fourth Cliff that afternoon, hoping to score a bird for Sunday dinner, but found that one of the boys had already left for home with the day's prizes, and that Webster was looking to leave as well. The other three boys stayed in the camp, a decision that would cost them dearly as the storm closed in on the South Shore, for as the storm grew, the waters of the North River rose.

The Clapps, farther downriver (on what is now known as the South River), fled their shanty for the safety of their small dory as the depth of the water steadily increased, but abandoned that when a runaway gundalow happened by. Luckily, it headed for shore in Marshfield, but not before passing within hearing distance of the screams of the Henderson boys, who were being swept away uncontrollably in their own dory. By the end of the week the bodies of George Ford, Albert Tilden and Bert and Fred Henderson were all found dead.

But the storm was after much more than just human lives.

Keeper Frederick Stanley reported in his log, "During the gale this day the flag pole was blown [down] the out-building was moved off from its foundation and a lot of shingles torn off, and the platforms were washed away with the steps of the station; and a key post with one key." The lifesaving station, at the southern end of the rise of Fourth Cliff, was under assault.

What came next might have been expected. In fact, one man, Reverend Samuel Deane, author of *History of Scituate, 1831*, practically predicted it half a century earlier. He wrote,

> The cliffs have gradually wasted by the attrition of the tides and storms. Comparing the third cliff with the number of acres of planting land originally laid out, we find that it is reduced nearly one half in two centuries. The fourth cliff wastes from twelve to fourteen

This stretch of sand between Third and Fourth Cliffs frustrated shipbuilders for decades. *Courtesy of Historical Research Associates.*

inches per annum. A large rock in front of the fourth cliff that now lies at low water mark, is remembered by many, to have been at the top of the cliff, two hundred feet above its present bed, and several feet within the edge of the precipice, half a century since. The other cliffs probably waste in the same proportion. The beach between the third and fourth cliff, is composed of sand and pebbles, and resists the attrition of the tides more than the cliffs; yet it is slowly wasting, and the river probably will eventually find its outlet between those cliffs.

Furthermore, he stated, the waters just behind that barrier beach, in what was then called New Harbour, might some day meet the sea whether Mother Nature had anything to say about it. "The fact that the River would form an excellent harbour," he wrote in 1831, "were it not for the shifting bar at its mouth, has given rise to various proposals for a remedy. It has often been in serious agitation, to cut a ship canal between the third and fourth cliffs; but the nature of the ground renders it probable that the same obstructions would there be met." Historian Lysander Salmon Richards, writing *History of Marshfield, Mass.* in 1901 from the Marshfield point of view, reiterated Deane's mention of the unstable mouth when he said, "The old mouth, within the memory of citizens now living, has shifted from time to time, at one time southerly from its present outlet and then northerly, so that the mouth during the past century has varied in its course from a half mile to a mile."

Richards, though, had the advantage of writing seventy years after Deane, and as such, had a lot more information to pass on regarding the river. He told the tale of an 1841 visit by then Representative John Quincy Adams to the proposed canal site between Third and Fourth Cliffs, and of how the authorities decided against the idea, fearing damage to the marshes.

> But nothing daunted a large party gathered together, and with picks, hoes, shovels, axes, etc., etc., with plenty of ox teams and horse teams to convey them, marched in the darkness of the night, with lanterns in hand to the beach, and there they began operations, dug and toiled throughout the vigils of the night. They dared not undertake the task in the day time, because it would be a criminal offense to be caught infringing against the rights of property vested in the United States.

The renegade "River Patriots" work party dug until water began to flow between the cliffs, but were dismayed to watch the passage silt its way shut again in a very short time. Richards also tells of a second attempt at artificial canal making, when "17 or 20 years after the first cut, another hole was made farther south, the southerly side of Fourth Cliff." Locals still alive at the time of Richards's writing who had participated in the second dig remembered being at it for three weeks or more, and doing it during the day, "having gained permission of the powers that be." Again, for a short time, water flowed through the cut until sand filled it back in again.

The fact that the canal was not dredged between the cliffs, and that a proposal that had actually reached Congress in 1829 for the formalization of a canal between the river mouth and Old Scituate Harbour had never been acted upon either, contributed to the end of shipbuilding on the North River. The trend toward larger ships left the builders in a bad position. Without the river being any deeper, as they supposed it would become with a wide opening between Third and Fourth Cliffs, they would never be able to keep up with the demand for large, modern wooden vessels. Faced with the inevitability of the situation, the last builder, Joseph Merritt, working at the Chittenden Yard, launched the ninety-ton *Helen M. Foster* in 1871, and then closed his doors for good.

Overnight on November 26–27, 1898, Mother Nature did what Samuel Deane had predicted she eventually would do. "A break had been blasted through the shingle beach and the course of the river dramatically altered," wrote Fred Freitas and David Ball in *Warnings Ignored! The Story of the Portland Gale, November, 1898*. Keeper Stanley of the Fourth Cliff Life-Saving Station entered in his journal that he now required a boat to cross where just a day earlier his men had walked across a sandy beach. "The break through the beach north of the station," wrote Ball and Freitas, "had made Humarock an island."

The old South River, which once flowed weakly from Center Marshfield to the outlet at Rexhame, gained about two miles in length. The North River lost those two miles, but increased in water level dramatically. In time, the old mouth of the river would silt its way shut.

Lysander Richards watched the progress of both mouths in the weeks and months after the storm. "When the new mouth was made by the great storm a little distance from the northerly end of the fourth Cliff, the old mouth began to partially fill up, and is now, in 1901, so filled up that teams can pass over it. It is a part of the beach, and continuous." In it, he saw the future, as, he stated, "It is undoubtedly open for all time."

Furthermore, he stated, "The river, as it approaches the new mouth is nearly a mile wide, and about ten feet deep. It has since widened, and is now some three or four hundred feet wide; at low tide about fourteen or sixteen feet deep. The current is very strong and rapid."

Upriver, in the days after the storm, the members of the North River Boat Club (of which Bert Henderson had been one) knew that changes were taking place. Sitting at the foot of the Union Street Bridge, the club had just celebrated its fifth anniversary. There would be no sixth. Water rushed into the building with each high tide. "After the storm," wrote Joseph Foster Merritt in *Anecdotes of the North River and South Shore*, "a few meetings were held but no social activities…Interest was gone and it seemed that it would not be possible again to enjoy sailing, owing to the changed conditions. A meeting was called September 8, 1899, to see what action the club would take towards raising or disposing of the boat house. It was voted to sell it at public auction."

In the days after the storm, the Duxbury and Cohasset Railroad could no longer roam over the mouth of the river, as, according to Richards, "the great storm, after the cut was made, washed away the railroad, passing over the marshes." The railroad moved quickly to replace the lost tracks. "It has since been replaced and raised a number of feet, and is now considered safe, although a very high tide, with an easterly storm, washes over it at times."

That inrush of water had one other significant impact on life on the river. While shipbuilders had long clamored for a deeper channel through which to navigate their newly built ships to sea, they did not necessarily understand what an influx of salt water would do to the ecology of the river, and to the livelihoods of the other people who depended upon it. The increased salinity level that resulted from the Portland Gale breakthrough killed off cedar tress close to the river's banks in marshy areas heretofore unaffected by salt water. Secondly, salt marsh haying, an ancient tradition on the North and South Rivers, ground to a halt, driving the final nail into the coffin of that already dying industry. Overnight, the North River became an entirely new habitat for man and beast alike.

In many ways, the North River has the Portland Gale to thank—or blame—for what it is today.

THE NORTH RIVER INDOORS

Numerous nonprofit organizations around the region are hard at work interpreting the cultural and natural history of the river; engaging locals in citizen science projects; educating the public about ecological concerns; and, most importantly, fiercely protecting the river from development, lawn chemical and automobile fuel and fluid infusions from storm drain runoffs, aquatic invasive species and habitat loss or misuse that could lead to the eradication of endangered native species of birds along the shores.

Two institutions, Norwell's South Shore Science Center and the Scituate Historical Society, are leading the way with modern museum exhibits featuring the opposite ends of the North River history spectrum. The science center, a vibrant, family learning-driven jewel of the South Shore, tackles the natural history of the North River marshes in its EcoZone, while the Scituate Historical Society's Maritime and Irish Mossing Museum has dedicated one of its six rooms entirely to the topic of shipbuilding on the North River. Both places allow visitors to become lost in thought and imagination as they step through the doors, one leading into nature and the other leading into the past.

The South Shore Natural Science Center and the EcoZone

Take a few steps to the left of the entryway into the South Shore Natural Science Center in Norwell and you have entered the EcoZone. A circular topographic map informs you of the world into which you are about to tread, that of the salt marshes of the North River watershed, and once you've traversed a short wooden bridge crossing a sphagnum moss bog, you're there.

To your right, a grand red maple tree stretches from the floor to the ceiling. Its branches reach over one pond full of spotted and wood turtles and another that's home to a bullfrog. And, if you're kid sized, you'll be able to climb inside a log that extends alongside both ponds and view all of these natural wonders, including swimming bluegills and sunfish, from under the water's surface.

Straight ahead of you are many more of the creatures that comfortably live in the local salt marshes, including an albino black rat snake, a garter snake, an eastern box

Jeff Corwin has dedicated significant volunteer time to make sure his hometown science center has a bright future ahead of it. Here, he joins local kids in a "tossing of the turtles" party, paving the way for a new exhibit. *Courtesy of South Shore Natural Science Center.*

turtle, spotted salamanders and wood and grey tree frogs, all in their own habitats, collectively composing the Creature Corner.

More than stepping into a museum exhibit, you have also just stepped into Jeff Corwin's childhood. Yes, that Jeff Corwin, the one who turned a generation of youngsters onto the world's wildlife on the Disney Channel program *Going Wild With Jeff Corwin* and now stars in and produces his own shows, *The Jeff Corwin Experience* and *Corwin's Quest* on Animal Planet. He's also the Jeff Corwin who grew up in the small town of Norwell and wandered in and out of the South Shore Natural Science Center as a kid.

"He was always in touch with what was going on at the science center, always involved, always in synch," said Martha Twigg, director of the center. She explained how Corwin, as a kid, would "push the envelope" while attending school. Having spent his youth in self-guided exploration of the open spaces near his home, "Who knew what he would bring in," said Twigg. Finally, his mother stressed to him the importance of learning all that he could about animals if he was going to be handling them.

A trip to the rainforests of Belize in 1984 accelerated his desire to learn more about the world's animals and strategies for their conservation. After earning bachelor of science degrees in biology and anthropology from Bridgewater State College and a master's of science in wildlife and fisheries conservation from UMass Amherst, Jeff became such an eloquent and informative advocate for global rainforest conservation that he was invited to address the General Assembly of the United Nations on the topic

The South Shore Natural Science Center is home to creatures in need of help, like Hedwig the barred owl, shown here on the arm of Jeff Corwin. © *2002 by Cary Wolinsky.*

in 1993. From there, his star rose through his television work on the Disney Channel. But he never forgot his roots.

"He walked into the science center in February 1999," said Twigg. "By that time he'd seen nature centers worldwide, and he had a germination of an idea of a vision brewing in his mind. He wanted kids to know that it could be just as exciting to go into your own backyard and interact with wildlife as it is to visit the places he does around the world."

The science center had not changed much from the days of Corwin's youth in the 1970s to the time he walked through the doors in 1999. Static exhibits had rarely moved and changed, and when they did, the process was time-consuming and laborious, without the visitation rewards they seemingly deserved for all the effort. A waterhole that never worked had become a sandbox.

"The place was dark and unfriendly," said Twigg. "But when Jeff talked to us about all the places he'd been, we got excited about the possibilities. How could we make the exhibits more interactive, educational and fun for everyone?"

A multi-pronged fundraising effort commenced within just a few short months. Disney underwrote three shows to be put on by Corwin at Cohasset's South Shore Music Circus that August. Norwell's Mt. Blue restaurant, partly owned at the time by rock band Aerosmith's Steven Tyler and Joe Perry, who are also South Shore residents, threw a summer party. Local artists headed by National Geographic photographer

The Scituate Maritime & Irish Mossing Museum stands out as one of the region's best small museums.

Cary Wolinsky collaborated on a series of frog paintings that became the artwork for the science center's "Peeper Pack" playing cards. When the dust settled, the board of directors and science center staff found themselves overwhelmed by people's generosity. About $160,000 had been raised.

The staff of the science center then set out on quests of their own, to visit regional nature centers and to seek potential designers to make Corwin's vision come to life. Corwin, although busy with his new partnership with Animal Planet, took the time to write down his thoughts during this process. "Jeff's stayed in focus," said Twigg. "We've never felt that if we had a question for him we couldn't approach him with it. He drops in from time to time unexpectedly and gives us his comments."

In January 2001, with the red maple tree in place, Corwin led a ceremonial "tossing of the turtles" party to introduce the turtles and frogs to their new homes. On June 13, 2002, he did two shows at Norwell High School, and on July 9, 2005, he joined Norwell-born blues artist Susan Tedeschi in hosting Wild Blue Night at the Music Circus. As funds continue to be raised, the EcoZone comes closer to completion. With homegrown help like Jeff Corwin around, still exploring the North River salt marshes from his home, that shouldn't be a problem.

Today, a sleeping squirrel can be viewed inside of a tree, while a perched raccoon looks down inquisitively from above. A vernal pool magically transforms from season to season at the push of a single button. And a sweeping mural offers a final view of the pastoral splendor of a North River meadow as one returns to the entryway.

The onus is then on the visitor. The introduction to nature has been made, and it's now time to see the real beauty of the North River marshes with a walk along a trail or a kayaking trip from one of its many launching spots.

The Scituate Maritime & Irish Mossing Museum

Don't try to read L. Vernon Briggs's 1889 *History of Shipbuilding on North River* in one sitting. It's like the Bible. It's full of useful information, but it's best taken in small snippets rather than as a forced narrative.

That said, do try to read *History of Shipbuilding on North River*. It's one book that will make your head spin when you try to gauge the length, breadth and depth of local history. And it's the one book that truly makes the reader understand that the North River, flowing through six towns, was in fact a community unto itself during those shipbuilding days of yore.

But before licking your fingertip and turning to page one, there's just one last thing you should do. Visit the Scituate Maritime & Irish Mossing Museum and let the Scituate Historical Society's docents give you a primer on the history you are about to learn.

The museum itself is in an old sea captain's home, belonging in 1739 to Captain Benjamin James, on the banks of a North River tributary. At one time it served as a smallpox hospital, and the accidental exhumation of several bodies across the street at the town's transfer station with telltale scars on their bones have corroborated this

The museum itself is an old Driftway home, approached through the kitchen ell.

historical fact. The historical society purchased the old home for refitting as a museum in 1995, opening it just a few years later as one of the premier small museums in the region.

The museum is divided into six main rooms. The old kitchen ell, through which visitors enter the building (the building faces the water, and therefore not the roadway and parking lot), features an orientation room and gift shop. The orientation room offers small samplings of all that will be seen in the other five main exhibits. The first floor is completed by the Shipwreck Room, Life-Saving Room and the Irish Mossing Room. Each room has an itinerant historical society–produced video that plays on a continual loop, and all are decorated with significant artifacts retrieved by divers, donated by descendants or purchased on internet auction websites. The society is always looking to add to and improve its collection.

The second floor is where the fun begins for North River buffs. The stairwell leading up to the two top-floor exhibits is lined with hand-drawn representations of North River views, all done in pencil and Sharpie marker by local artist, musician and schoolteacher Skip Toomey. At the top of the stairs a door opens to the coziness of a typical parlor that may have been in the home of any Scituate sea captain, with period furniture, nineteenth-century position finding instruments (sextants and octants), paintings and photographs of Scituate men who went to sea and even hand-carved wooden toy furniture made on those long voyages.

But, of course, before they could go to sea, these captains had to have ships on which to sail. Around the corner from the Ship Captains' Room one steps through a short corridor, past what was the front-door stairwell, to find the North River Shipbuilding Room. Looking directly into the far corner, the eye is drawn past a tool bench stocked with adzes and hammers and out the window into a North River shipyard, where shipwrights are hard at work on their latest creation. The scene is meant to be generic, and it is. It could be any one of the family-owned yards along the banks from the North River Bridge to the sea.

According to Briggs,

> Prior to 1800 North River was known the world over; vessels were not designated as having been built in Scituate, Marshfield, Hanover or Pembroke, but "on North River." The author has unearthed the records of over one thousand and twenty-five vessels built here, and the United States Flag was carried around the world, and among other places, to the following countries for the first time at the mast heads of North River built vessels: Great Britain, Canada, the Northwest coast, to the Black Sea and China.

Furthermore, he states, the river shipyards peaked around the year 1800:

> The largest number of vessels built on the River in a single year that the author has found the records of was thirty in 1801, and the year 1818 shows the next largest number, twenty-four. During the five years from 1799 to 1804 inclusive, there were built here one hundred and fifteen vessels, an average of twenty-three each year. During the ten years from 1794–1804 inclusive, there were one hundred and seventy-eight vessels built here, or an average of seventeen each year.

And, he says, the shipbuilders tended to think alike at times. "The largest number of vessels found bearing the same name were Betseys and Sallys, fourteen each; twelve Marys, eleven Pollys, and ten Neptunes."

On the wall opposite the workbench a map, also hand drawn and stylized by Skip Toomey, shows the North River as it looked prior to 1898, from its upriver anchor works to the fitting-out station at White's Ferry. Each shipyard is named and placed on the map, giving the viewer an excellent chance to ruminate in the manner in which Henry F. Howe did in *Salt Rivers of the Massachusetts Shore* in 1951:

> The North River yards were as great an anomaly in their day as is Scotland's Clyde today, for one broods over the narrow winding stream meandering down through its salt marshes with sheer wonder that 400-ton ships could be got to sea along that route, just as one gazes in consternation at the shipyard of the great Cunard queens on its little river now. Yet in this Federalist period an average of twenty-three vessels were completed each year in North River yards. Eleven shipyards were in view from the Hanover bridge eight miles from the sea, with twelve more downstream. Now only a few old retaining walls remain of all that century-long activity.

Howe's wondrousness at the situation is well-founded, for the snaking river, especially prior to the Portland Gale of 1898, did not enjoy the idea of giving up its shipyard creations that easily. River pilots, who barked orders to oxen team drivers ashore from the decks of new ships, did their best to drive the vessels along through shallow, narrow passages, hauling the vessels up onto kedge anchors thrown forward as guideposts. As eloquently put by Howe,

> One stands now among the scrubby oak and tupelo that have overgrown the old shipways, and can scarcely dream up the vision of the old ox teams, the busy clatter of adze and calking iron, or the excited pageantry of a launching. It is almost beyond the power of imagination to visualize gangs of men hauling a newly-launched hull with ropes, now "over to Sit-u-wate," now "over to Ma'ashfield," to avoid the shoals at the windings of the placid little streams.

The "Sit-u-wate" and "Ma'ashfield" calls were of supreme importance, as not every young man of the day had been schooled to today's standards, meaning he may not know right from left, north from south or east from west. But being a local boy, he sure knew the difference between Scituate and Marshfield. Briggs tells of a local pilot, called "Old Neptune," known to swear a ship from Barstow's Yard to the old mouth or, to put it more softly, who "used to give his orders in the imperative mood." The imagined scene is priceless. Foul language flying from the pilot's mouth to the ears of those ox team drivers, their whips cracking in fear that they be singled out for individual abuse and before long the newest *Betsey* or *Sally* is surfing its way toward the open ocean. Examining the map on the wall at the museum, one can pick out what must have been those tough spots through which to fight, and can almost hear Old Neptune shouting, "Pull away there on starboard bow!" with "the torpedo snap that made the command tingle with authority."

The map in the Shipbuilding Room holds one extra feature that makes learning the story of North River shipbuilding days that much easier. Today's North River boater will notice the representation of a barrier beach stretching from Third Cliff to Fourth Cliff, across what is now the mouth of the North River. As stated earlier, the mouth has moved. Originally it sat about two and a half miles to the south-southeast of its current position, near Rexhame Beach. Seeing the thinness of the old barrier beach and the extra distance through which pilots had to force their ships, one can understand why in the 1800s the shipbuilders pleaded with the federal government to cut a canal between the aforementioned cliffs. The government never obliged, and shipbuilding on the river died. In 1898, perhaps poetically, Mother Nature made the change herself through the power of the Portland Gale.

The end of shipbuilding on the North River is symbolized by a photograph blown up and graphically presented on the western wall of the Shipbuilding Room, the image of the schooner *Helen M. Foster* at its launching from the Chittenden Yard in 1871. It was the last ship of notable size so constructed in the river's history.

Leaving the room offers the perfect chance to pause at the stairwell off the corridor between it and the Ship Captains' Room. On the far wall are silhouettes of the various types of vessels built in North River yards, but on the side walls run three long exhibit panels that list the names of every ship built on the river—every *Mary*, every *Polly*, every *Neptune*.

PROTECTING THE RIVER

The North and South Rivers Watershed Association

It's relatively easy to get behind the preservation of historic buildings. They're everywhere on the South Shore, from ancient taverns, like the Old Ordinary in Hingham, to historic towers, like Lawson's Tower or Scituate Lighthouse in that coastal community, to quaint homes like the Harlow Old Fort House in Plymouth or the Major John Bradford Homestead in Kingston. They have familiar human stories to tell, they have obvious and understandable needs, like new roofs, and they're often in well-known, historic neighborhoods we pass through every day. They're beloved members of small communities.

Try to apply the same thoughts to the protection of a river. The clues to the human history that bind us to the story of a river are often fleeting (like a wooden workboat rotting in a marsh, covered by invasive grasses that obscure it in summer) or they're simply gone, like the sounds of the saws that cut the wood that built the ships launched from the river's banks just more than a century ago. And the needs of the river are not the needs of the average citizen, like regulations enforcing protection from storm water runoff and the chemicals it can carry from roadways into the water. And for the most part, rivers are only ever noticed by those folks who live along their banks or have some specific recreational use for them in mind. Thousands of people drive across the Route 3A and Route 3 bridges between Marshfield and Scituate and Norwell and Pembroke every single day, yet few give the North River and its conservation needs a conscious thought.

Now, try to envision applying the same preservation or conservation ethos to the protection of an entire watershed. Now you can begin to understand the challenges facing the one hundred or so watershed associations across Massachusetts, organizations charged with restoring or ensuring the continued health of all the lands that drain into all the ponds, lakes and estuaries that feed the river of choice.

The North and South Rivers Watershed Association (NSRWA), for instance, deals with an expanse of land that encompasses sections of twelve South Shore towns. Some of those relationships are obvious: Marshfield, Scituate, Norwell, Hanover and Pembroke directly abut the river's banks. Yet drainage issues in seven other communities—Hingham, Weymouth, Rockland, Abington, Whitman, Hanson and Duxbury—affect

Water-skiing and powerboating used to take place up and down the North River. Regulations now prohibit water-skiing and keep boats to no-wake speeds. *Courtesy of Scituate Historical Society.*

the waters of the North and South Rivers. It takes real "big picture" thinking to see the problems facing an entire watershed, as compared to those of just the rivers proper.

As Samantha Woods, executive director of the NSRWA, puts it, "The tributaries are just as important as the river. You wouldn't want to clog up the veins any more than you do the heart."

America's first watershed association, the Brandywine Valleys Association in Pennsylvania, formed in 1945, but it took a while for the conservation bug to catch on in such a manifestation on the South Shore. In 1969, a Scituate birder named Jean Foley noticed a diminishing number of a certain species of sparrow in the marshes along the North River, places where they had historically been in abundance. She wondered whether recent development along Scituate's Driftway could be partially to blame, so she contacted town hall with her concerns. When the town leaders failed to respond to her questions, she went public with her apprehensions about the future of the natural spaces she so loved. She and her husband Jack hosted a meeting of environmentalists, members of local conservation commissions and other interested parties in the spring of 1970, and from that gathering grew the North and South Rivers Watershed Association, which today is fifteen hundred members strong.

A protective mother piping plover will feign injuries to draw attention away from her eggs.

There were some early successes for the organization, like achieving federal designation as a National Natural Landmark for both rivers in 1977 (just one of eleven such appellations in all of Massachusetts) and a Protective Order for the North River under the state Scenic Rivers Act of 1971, enacted a year later in 1978. This move provided for the formation of the North River Commission, a body composed of citizens from the five towns bordering the river and dedicated to regulating development along the river's edge.

Yet as gung-ho as the founders were their energy eventually waned, and the North and South Rivers Watershed Association fell into a period of relative stasis through the early 1980s. It took a key environmental debate—some would say that "battle" is not too strong a word—to reinvigorate the group and give it its "second wind," according to Woods. "The Scituate Wastewater Treatment Plant was basically running an illegal outfall on the Herring River," she says, "and the association went to war." The organization brought suit against the Town of Scituate, forcing the community to focus on and alter its operation of the facility. "Now it's one of the cleanest run plants of its kind in the state," says Woods.

The Scituate Wastewater Treatment Plant fight led to a renaissance for the organization. With new board members and, for the first time, a paid director, the North and South Rivers Watershed Association moved forward with initiatives aimed at cleaner water, increased recreational access, public education and conservation partnerships with the communities bordering the rivers.

Standing on the North River Bridge on the Hanover-Pembroke line, one can look downriver to where once a dozen shipyards rang with activity.

Today, the association boasts a payroll of four and a host of ongoing projects targeting mission goals to protect the watershed, educate the public and restore the health of the water and the contiguous watershed habitats. For instance, there's the River Watch Water Quality Testing Program, through which volunteers test fecal coliform bacteria levels at ten sites throughout the summer. Throughout the winter, the association joins with the South Shore Natural Science Center and Mass Audubon's South Shore Sanctuaries in producing free Wednesday night lectures in the "Water Watch" series, covering subjects ranging from hardcore science to local history, all having to do with the topic of water. The NSRWA also serves as the South Shore partner of the Massachusetts Bays Program, a federal program that works to conserve the health of the entirety of Massachusetts Bay. Since becoming the South Shore Mass Bays' partner in 2001, the NSRWA has leveraged more than $3 million in funding for environmental projects on the South Shore.

In addition, the NSRWA hosts high-profile events meant to engage the public, like the annual "River Views" house tour of homes along the rivers' edges, offering tour-goers the chance to see the North and South Rivers from angles they might never otherwise have access to; and the Great River Race, a chase upriver from the Union Street Bridge to the old Washington Street Bridge that's open to anybody on anything propelled by paddles. And then there are more targeted efforts, like encouraging local communities to adopt

In 1919, the North River
Historical Society marked the
sites of the historic shipyards.

the Community Preservation Act in order to protect important watershed land (Scituate, Marshfield, Hanover, Norwell and Pembroke have all adopted it), reducing storm water pollution to the rivers and working to restore fish habitats and herring runs in areas where old dams and other impediments keep fish from reaching their historic spawning grounds upriver. For example, according to the association, where once there was a robust herring run, now Scituate's First Herring Brook hasn't seen a herring in years, in part due to the lack of flow management over the dams and the competing use of the water for public supply.

Woods sees even one-on-one interaction with members of the public to be of potential benefit to the future of the river. "If we can engage people at the local level to feel empowered and educated that they can do something, then they will speak out at Town Meeting or in other forums," she says. "Most people want to do the right thing by the environment, and if you give them the right tools, they can do it."

In the end, one realizes that the North and South Rivers—and the watersheds that serve them—are not so unlike Marshfield's Winslow House or Duxbury's King Caesar House. Shipbuilders launched more than one thousand vessels from the rivers' banks between 1690 and 1871, when the rivers were communities unto themselves. Salt

The base of Cornhill Lane, which once launched that rarest of ships, the snow brig, offers striking scenery.

marsh hay gatherers filled untold numbers of gundalows with that useful product, and millwrights harnessed the power of the rivers' tributaries to saw wood and grind corn. Pollution, in its general sense, is something we all understand, and thanks to the work of local conservation commissions, nonprofit environmental organizations and state and federal conservation initiatives, access to the natural beauty of the North and South Rivers is on the increase. The members of the North and South Rivers Watershed Association believe that like those historic homes, the rivers, tributaries, lakes and ponds, too, can once again become beloved members of the South Shore communities.

The North River Commission and the Massachusetts Scenic River Designation

Lloyd Vernon Briggs of Hanover was a standout American, as well as a remarkable man of the South Shore. An alumnus of the Hanover Academy at Hanover Four Corners, he planned to study medicine, but a diagnosis of tuberculosis sent his life spinning into another direction in his early years. At seventeen, in 1880, he sailed around Cape Horn to Hawaii and back, hoping the salubriousness of the open sea would revive him. It apparently did, as he lived a long and productive life, dying in 1941. Among his accomplishments were several genealogical works, religious histories, the adoption of the Briggs Law in Massachusetts—providing for the automatic psychiatric evaluation of those accused of a serious crime—and the co-chairmanship of the panel charged with determining the mental status of Leon Czolgosz, the man who murdered President William McKinley.

And by the time he was twenty-six, L. Vernon Briggs Jr. had researched and written the 421 pages of *History of Shipbuilding on North River*. To compile that much information in the days before the internet meant dozens, if not hundreds, of personal interviews, poring through dusty tomes of financial records, scouring diaries, delving into family Bibles and numerous semi-archaeological site investigations. In short, it took real, classic historian's research skills to compile the book. As such, Briggs was someone who had seen the river like no one else ever had, from the perspective of just about everybody who ever used it for anything for the first two hundred years of European settlement.

His love of the river and his desire for protection comes through in the opening pages of his book on the subject: "Until 1628," he wrote, "the waters of the North River had probably never been disturbed by any navigator excepting the Indian in his canoe, and how we all would like to look back three hundred years and see the same beautiful river with the picturesque Indian and canoe, he disturbing the quiet waters with the silent dipping of his paddle." Even in 1889, Briggs yearned for a return to nature for the North River, for the inherent beauty of the waterway to stand free from the steadily marching encroachment of civilization.

It was in that same spirit in the 1970s, as we have seen earlier in this chapter, that the North and South Rivers Watershed Association agitated for the designation of the North River as a Scenic and Recreational River. In some form, Briggs's vision for the future of the river would come true.

The Scenic and Recreational River Protective Order for the North River came in nineteen pages under the state's acts of 1978, through the Department of Environmental Management (now part of the Department of Conservation and Recreation). The order has twelve sections, of which the first is the most important:

> *The Commissioner of Environmental Management, acting pursuant to G.L. c. 21, s. 17B and c. 367, s. 62 of the Acts of 1978, for the purposes of promoting the public safety, health and welfare, and protecting public and private property, wildlife, freshwater fisheries, and irreplaceable wild, scenic and recreational river resources, hereby adopts this Order establishing the North River Commission…and regulating, restricting or prohibiting uses and activities in the Scenic and Recreational River Corridor along both the North River and parts of associated tributaries in the towns of Scituate, Marshfield, Pembroke, Norwell, Hanover and Hanson in the County of Plymouth.*

The new commission, made up of one member and one alternate appointed by the selectmen of each of the six towns bordering the river, took the responsibility of creating a set of bylaws under which the commission would operate, and several other tasks: project reviews, special permit reviews, order violations investigations, collection of filing fees, etc. In other words, the group became the watchdogs that would ensure there was no inappropriate construction or other use of the land near the river that could harmfully affect the water corridor in any way. And that was a big task.

The protective order details allowable existing uses of structures along the corridor. Buildings, for instance, along the river that need repair may be repaired, but they may not be added onto without a special permit from the commission. Buildings torn down can be rebuilt, but only to a size no larger than their predecessors, and so on. Section five lists the allowed uses, most of which have to comply with site design restrictions and chemical application requirements. Motorboat owners, according to the order, must keep their vessels at or below six miles per hour, or no-wake headway speed. Racing is prohibited, and "Waterskiing shall not be permitted on the River."

This last statement came not just as a just-in-case, throw-in restriction. Writer Fessenden S. Blanchard, who qualified the river as one of his *Ghost Towns of New England* in his book of that name, told of his visit to the river in the 1950s on a boat chartered from Mary's Boat Livery in the shadow of the Route 3A, or Little's, Bridge:

> *This time I ran the river with my wife, Mary, in an outboard runabout piloted by a pretty fourteen-year-old girl named Jane Williams, who banked our boat steeply as we rounded the bends at almost full speed and nonchalantly waved at various youthful swains who passed us going equally fast in the other direction. "We do a lot of water skiing around here," she said, as we tried hard to imagine what the river was like in the days before it became an outboard paradise.*

The most impressive list in the order, though, is the register of prohibited uses, among which are new airports or landing strips, nuclear generating facilities, communication towers, gas stations, auto graveyards, mobile home parks, hospitals, indoor rinks, dams and signs, "including any outdoor sign, display, notice, placard, poster, billboard or any other device intended or used to advertise of inform, except Commission signs, official historic markers, official land use, traffic and boat traffic signs, or any signs less than $3\frac{1}{2}$ X $3\frac{1}{2}$ which are not visible from the river or any bridge crossing the river." There can be no storage of hazardous waste, no dumping of snow and no discharge of pollutants unless allowable by federal or state law. By July 1980, the Department of Environmental Management had released the North River Management Plan, defining the boundaries of the corridor and outlining suggested land, water and recreation management practices town by town, further strengthening the commission's role in protecting the river.

Were he alive today, L. Vernon Briggs would be proud to know that such steps have been taken to protect the river he loved so much.

The Important Bird Area Designation

Every waterway attracts wildlife, be they four-legged and furry (or scaly), or two-legged and feathery. Yet some waterways, because of their positioning on the planet relative to annual avian migration patterns, the abundance of food they offer both beneath their surface and along their banks or the specialized nesting habitat they provide, attract more wildlife than others, or attract species that are specifically reliant on those exceptional offerings. Yes, the North River is one of those waterways. For several reasons, former director of Mass Audubon's South Shore Sanctuaries David Clapp and Scott Hecker, director of Coastal Bird Conservation for the National Audubon Society, nominated the North River Mouth and Corridor for designation as one of Massachusetts's seventy-nine Important Bird Areas.

According to Mass Audubon, an Important Bird Area, or IBA, "is a site providing essential habitat to one or more species of breeding, wintering, and/or migrating birds." The IBA movement began in Europe in 1985, when BirdLife International, a global affiliation of conservation organizations in more than one hundred countries, set out to accomplish four goals:

> To identify, nominate, and designate key sites that contribute to the preservation of significant bird populations or communities; to provide information that will help land managers evaluate areas for habitat management and/or land acquisition; to activate public and private participation in bird conservation efforts; and, to provide public education and community outreach opportunities.

By 2000, the partnership had designated 3,400 IBAs in Europe alone. The movement reached the United States in 1995 and, since that time, forty-six states have joined the cause, identifying 1,500 IBAs around the country.

Massachusetts picked up the gauntlet in 2000 and set to work to identify the state's most precious avian hotspots. Nominations closed in December 2002, and those aforementioned seventy-nine sites were selected, including the North River Mouth and Corridor. Other sites on the South Shore include Wompatuck State Park in Hingham, Cohasset and Norwell; Mass Audubon's Daniel Webster Wildlife Sanctuary and the town of Marshfield's conservation land at Cherry Hill; and Plymouth and Duxbury Bays and Ellisville Harbor in Plymouth.

So what makes the North River (and parts of the South River) Mouth and Corridor so important for our feathered friends? Well, it depends on which bird you ask.

Two species that are listed as endangered—the piping plover, listed federally, and the least tern, endangered in Massachusetts—are dependent upon sandy beaches for their nests. The plovers, noted for their hornpipe-like peep, require stretches of soft sand in which to lay their eggs, while the terns prefer a slightly more chaotic landscape, using rockier stretches higher up barrier beaches to hide their clutches. Both nests end up being quite well naturally disguised, blending in magnificently with their surroundings, making for an interesting early season's search for conservationists from Mass Audubon's Coastal Waterbird Program looking to find, monitor and protect them.

These birds in particular face two major foes when attempting to raise their young. Spring storms that bring higher than normal tides can wash out the nests of both species. Audubon staff members have watched in disbelief as mothers-to-be have physically rolled their eggs up the beach from encroaching waters. The birds can renest, and several times, but female plovers, for instance, will eventually reach a point of no return. If her last clutch is laid too late in the season, she may not have enough time to both raise her young and gain the appropriate amount of fat needed to make her way south for the winter.

The second opponent to these birds, sadly, is us. The area off Third Cliff known as "The Spit" to many local residents is a highly popular recreation spot in summertime, and why not? It's got sand, sun, water and access to the open sea for those with big enough boats willing to challenge the surf at the mouth of the river. But while young people are throwing footballs and running through the sand on the Fourth of July, those tiny eggs are extremely vulnerable to destruction and the tenuous futures of the endangered birds are at risk. Mass Audubon, in cooperation with the Town of Scituate, oversees the placement and maintenance of "symbolic fencing" around fragile areas, essentially roping off the birds from the revelers. Unfortunately, that deterrent is not always enough. Maliciousness, often fueled by drunkenness, leads to the loss of eggs and the perpetuation of the endangered species designation for the birds.

Other species make abundant use of the North River Mouth and Corridor as well. Those same flats on which the plovers and terns nest each spring are also significant staging areas for migratory shorebirds, including vanishing populations of red knots (a bird struggling to survive because of the overharvesting of horseshoe crabs to the south, which has left historic feeding grounds relatively devoid of its chosen food, horseshoe crab eggs). Upriver, cattail marshes support both marsh wrens and salt marsh sharp-tailed sparrows, while wading birds such as great and snowy egrets and green, great blue, little blue and black-crowned night herons nab their prey in the marshes. Those same salt marshes provide food for northern harriers that glide slowly over the grass tops, ready to pounce on meadow voles and field mice. Some wintering ducks find seasonal peace in the calmer waters of the river, while others, like common eiders and surf and white-winged scoters, loaf in rafts either just inside or just outside the breakers. Double-crested (summer) and great cormorants (winter) enjoy the many docks and floats on which to stand and spread out their wings to dry.

At the moment, the designation of the North River Mouth and Corridor as an IBA comes without any protective legislation, or "teeth." But it does provide an important steppingstone toward protection. According to Wayne Petersen, Mass Audubon's IBA program director,

> Mass Audubon is currently working cooperatively with interested parties to develop conservation plans for future habitat management on designated sites. In some cases, efforts will be made to include IBAs in the state's open space planning program. In other cases conservation easements or a modification in land management practices may be recommended. The primary objective will be to facilitate whatever strategy works best for the site as well as to ensure the future protection of the site as an Important Bird Area.

The road ahead may be a long one, but at least now bird lovers along the river have a map to go by.

Driving the Rivers

So you've got one week's vacation this summer you've looked forward to all year long, and you plan on visiting the North and South Rivers. You plan to walk every trail you can find, to rent a kayak and watch the sunset.

But it's raining.

You needn't worry, for the North and South Rivers can be enjoyed from the comfort of your own car. What follow are the best vistas of the river available to those folks who, for one reason or another, choose to see the rivers from behind the wheel.

North River Bridge

If a stop atop the North River Bridge on the Washington Street boundary between Pembroke and Hanover doesn't pique historical curiosity about the North River in the visitor, then nothing will. Here, history can be reenacted. Stand on the bridge, look downriver and imagine the dozen shipyards at work in 1800. Step aside momentarily to let the Boston to Plymouth stagecoach rumble through, or be prepared to evacuate at the advance of the war games combatants of 1909. Listen for the saws and adzes. Watch for the sliding of the *Mary* down the ways back toward the bridge on the right, or Pembroke, side of the river from Thomas Turner's shipyard.

Step back even farther in time by looking down from the western side of the bridge and spying the abutments of William Barstow's earliest bridge, small piles of rocks that once supported the small crossing that helped the earliest settlers keep their feet dry as they went about their work on the river.

A short stop around the corner brings about the chance to reflect on another moment of the river's history, that of the days when historians began marking the ancient shipbuilding spots. Take Washington Street into Hanover, and take the first right onto Old Bridge Road. The road was named for not the famous North River Bridge, but rather for the Rainbow Bridge, an ancient footbridge over Third Herring Brook.

Taking a right onto Old Shipyard Lane, turn around in the dead end, and on the way back out look for the sign erected on the right by the North River Historical Association in 1919 on the site of Smith's, and later Barstow's, yards. Some of these signs are now horribly rusted, while others, like the Fox Hill Yard sign at Barque Hill in Norwell, have been lovingly maintained.

If ever there was a nonprofit organization that should be revived, it's the North River Historical Association.

Route 3 South Overpass

Modern engineering has provided some magnificent things for this world, in the form of towering skyscrapers that offer the average human being the ability to fly with his or her feet on the ground, to see the world below as only a bird can naturally, from dozens of stories in the sky. And engineers have designed bridges that transport us across canals and bays, and even to islands to which we once could only sail.

It's a shame, though, that engineers had the ability to build Route 3 South when they did. It's almost an exercise in creative fantasy writing to try to imagine what that stretch of the river would look like today without it. While approaching Exit 13 from the south, the view downriver is simply breathtaking. The wide corridor is heavily fringed with salt marsh, and the trees along the banks look as if they're being seen by human eyes for the first time. It's a National Park–type feeling to gaze upon it.

The one standout geological feature of the area is the hill that today is behind the rest area just to the north of the river, on the Norwell side. Historically, the area was known as the Bald Hills, the scene of at least some shipbuilding carried on by John Stetson, who also built an early mill at Scituate Harbor. But this does not answer the one burning question all want answered: where did the name "Bald Hills" come from?

L. Vernon Briggs in *History of Shipbuilding on North River* gives several theories, including the notion that dances, or balls, were once held on this high point overlooking the river. He also notes that the Hanover artillery used the Pembroke side for target practice from this point, firing balls across the river toward the Brick Kiln area. In the end, though, he relies on an anecdote passed on by a local, John Tower, who "when very young he asked an old man why it was called 'Bald Hill,' which he always understood to be the name, and he replied by taking off his hat, and rubbing his smooth pate with has hand, saying, it was because it was as destitute of trees as his head was of hair." That may have been the case in those days. Today the eminence is covered with natural growth, mostly of the tallest kind.

Brick Kiln Lane

The most important thing to remember when driving the rivers is to respect the privacy of the people who own homes along its banks. In most cases, they bought or built their residences for much the same reason you're driving the streets on which they're situated: they enjoy the beauty of the river.

Brick Kiln Lane in Pembroke is the site of one of the most famous North River–built ships of all time. Pembroke split off from Duxbury in 1712 and incorporated as its own town, and within two decades, as far back as all known records tell us, shipbuilding became a major concern. The Turner family—Captain Benjamin, Captain Ichabod Sr., Captain Ichabod Jr. and Calvin (who apparently never got his captain's license)—built ships here between 1730 and 1807 at the Brick Kiln Yard.

Ichabod Sr. had oversight of the yard during the years leading up to and just after the American Revolution, from 1764 to 1787 or 1788. His projects included the brig *Norfolk* and ships *Neptune* and *Lima* before he constructed the ship *Beaver*, that most famous of all. Even if the ship's name has not been carried down through time in the textbooks of American schoolchildren, the name of the event to which it is attached certainly has been: the Boston Tea Party.

Beaver was one of four ships that set sail from London for Boston on October 18, 1773. Three of them, *Beaver*, *Dartmouth* and *Eleanor*, made it to the city. The fourth, *William*, wrecked on the inside of Cape Cod, a total loss before making it to Griffin's Wharf. On December 16, outraged citizens of Boston stormed the three ships, hauled out the cargo of tea recently transported across the Atlantic and tossed it into the sea in the name of freedom from taxation without representation. This event added fuel to the growing fire that would eventually engulf the colonies in their war of rebellion against British rule.

The original *Beaver* sailed to England again in 1774 and there it remained, sold upon the death of its captain. But memories of the small brig need not be lost. The Boston Tea Party Historical Society keeps the history alive while the Boston Tea Party Ships and Museum is hard at work renovating its exhibits after a damaging fire. The *Brig Beaver II*, a re-creation of the original, is being renovated in Gloucester for future use when the museum reopens on Congress Street in Boston.

But if that's too far of a drive for this day's exploration, follow Brick Kiln Lane for a few hundred yards, past the grand home and farm of the Thomases. The road will turn sharply to the left (if you see a llama, you've gone too far), but before it does, look down and to the right, toward the river. In the woods at the base of the slope, there's an indent in the ground where, most likely, the original brig *Beaver* launched on its way to immortality.

Cornhill Lane

Following Union Street through Marshfield, when coming off Route 139, is like eating a bowl of ice cream after being fed a bowl of gruel. The stressful congestion of a major thoroughfare is given up for a country road past open farmland and ancient farmhouses. Such is the character of Two Mile and North Marshfield.

Along that road, as it rises to a crest of one of the many rolling hills of the village, Cornhill Lane appears on the left. That road descends gently toward the river, rounding a tight final turn before coming to a stop in a cul-de-sac at almost water level. You've arrived at the site of the Rogers Shipyard and Gravelly Beach.

The Rogerses built ships at two sites on the river, here and farther downstream at Little's Bridge. L. Vernon Briggs offered high praise for the family when he said of them, "The Rogers were skilled ship-carpenters, and if any one wanted a ship built on honor, a Rogers was his man."

This yard launched an oddity of American maritime history, a snow brig, the *Pacific Trader*, on July 27, 1796. Snow brigs (pronounced "snoo") had fore- and mainmasts and a small snow mast directly behind the main. The fore- and main-masts were square rigged, meaning their sails were large squares or rectangles flying perpendicular to the masts, while the snow mast flew a trysail, a fore-and-aft rigged, triangular sail. Snows or snow brigs saw service in the merchant trade from the Revolution onward, and sometimes saw military service. The brigs *Niagara* and *Lawrence*, combatants during the War of 1812, sported snow rigging, as does the sail training ship *Niagara* operated by the Erie Maritime Museum today.

The view from the end of Cornhill Lane spectacularly shows off a little-known Mass Audubon parcel, the thirteen-acre Chase-Garceau Wildlife Sanctuary, directly across the river. Downriver, the site of the Wanton Yard can be seen, without any discerning landmarks. While in the area, at all times of year, scan the marsh and shrubs for birds. During summer, double-crested cormorants can be seen swimming in the river, diving for fish.

Chittenden Lane

Cruising down the long, straight roadway of Chittenden Lane, one gets the sensation that something has to be wrong, that there's no way the North River could be this far off River Street. Don't give up hope.

But do remember that parking at the town-owned landing is restricted to Norwell residents only. The journey, though, for local historians, is worth the inconvenience of staying in the car for a moment and soaking in the historical significance, for it was on this spot in 1871 that the *Helen M. Foster*, the last of the North River–built ships, was launched.

Bridge Street/Union Street

The view from this bridge may change in years to come, as it's due for some major repair work. But that does not mean one should stop on the bridge to enjoy the view by any means. The road is heavily traveled, and usually at speeds higher than recommended, so the bridge is a busy spot. Parking momentarily at the Norwell Canoe Launch allows for views downriver, directly on the spot of the old North River Boat Club. Across the bridge in the Marshfield Canoe Launch area, the site of the Brooks-Tilden shipyard, a few steps out of the car brings one right to the river's edge. Look upstream here to try to make out the distant Rapids. At the next bend in the river back from the bridge stood the Block House Yard.

Directly across from the Brooks-Tilden Yard the remains of an ancient vessel rot away in the marsh, either a gundalow or a boat used by the North River Boat Club, as mentioned by Joseph Foster Merritt in *Anecdotes of the North River and South Shore*.

Riverside Circle

It's foolish, of course, to say that there is no history connected to any piece of land along the North River, but that can almost be said about the stretch that runs alongside the base of Riverside Circle in Marshfield. The Clift family owned a home built in 1702 on Spring Street at about the site of today's entrance to Riverside Circle. According to Cynthia Krusell and Betty Magoun Bates's *Marshfield: A Town of Villages*, Joseph Clift Sr. was born in that house and ran a store in it from 1765 to about 1800, taking time off to fight in the American Revolution. In 1797, he moved to Two Mile, where he bought and remodeled a house owned by—you guessed it—the Hatch family.

Riverside Circle offers a wide, sweeping view of one of the last twists in the river before it widens at the Union Street Bridge. There is no place to park in the area, but a slow ride along the street never hurt anybody. Please remember to respect the privacy of the local residents when you drive through.

Route 3A Bridge

Doggett's Ferry, Little's Bridge, Sergeant Michael Jason Kelley Memorial Bridge, whatever you want to call it, this crossing has long afforded spectacular views of the last eastward-running section of the North River. In times recently past, enjoying the view has been difficult, but the 2001 completion of the bridge renovation project came with a turnoff and rest area on the southbound side. Red-tailed hawks often perch in the trees alongside the road, and in summer great and snowy egrets stalk the marshes spearing small fish, frogs or whatever else wiggles unwittingly into their view.

A to Z Boatworks on the Scituate side and Mary's Boat Yard on the Marshfield side bracket the bridge, the latter site being where the rest of the Rogers family, mentioned above, built their ships from 1784 to 1809.

Damon's Point

As soon as you round Murdock's (or Lewis's) Pond and set your wheels on Damon's Point Road, you've landed yourself on the old rail bed of the Duxbury and Cohasset Railroad. Sadly, the story of the railroad is one of big business bullying local town leaders, as described by both Lysander Salmon Richards and Joseph C. Hagar. According to Richards, "A great effort was made by the citizens of East Marshfield to have it run through the middle of the village locating the station somewhere in the station of what is known as 'Bear's Brook,' by the road leading over it from Rodger's Corner to Sea View." East Marshfield is today's Marshfield Hills and Beare's Brook (named for early settlers Richard and Grace Beare) runs roughly along Prospect Street and is crossed by Pleasant Street, which runs out to Sea View.

The Old Colony Railroad countered by designing a shore route, one that could be used to hopefully attract Bostonians to partake of the beauty of the seaside at Sea View, Rexhame, Ocean Bluff and Brant Rock. In the end, after Marshfield shelled out $75,000 to build it (with more from Duxbury and Scituate), the road failed as an enterprise. The Old Colony then offered to buy the road for $15,000, splitting that money three ways amongst the towns. "This left Marshfield with a debt of $70,000," said Richards, "and it has been groaning under this incubus for years."

The last train ran in 1939, and Joseph C. Hagar gave its eulogy. "The road may have started with the application of the worst principles of capitalism; it has all ended in bankruptcy!" he said. "But to the credit of the road, it must be said that it built up Marshfield to a prosperous condition of a summer sea side resort for the people of Boston and Plymouth County."

Follow Damon's Point to the end today and you can look into the distance and watch as the rest of the old bed runs away into Scituate. The area is particularly of interest to bird-watchers, both for the abundance of birdhouses kept by a local resident and the salt marsh surrounding the view. Belted kingfishers loudly chatter as they fly from snag to pier and greater yellowlegs sound their *kew-kew-kew* call in company with shorebirds of all types in migration, while farther downstream, near the mouth, gulls, cormorants and terns gather on the Spit.

Humarock

It's still hard for newcomers to grasp the idea that you have to leave Scituate, go through Marshfield for several miles and cross the Sea Street or Julian Street Bridge to get back into Scituate again. But that's life on the Humarock peninsula, that most odd of oddities, a peninsula that once connected to the Scituate side and had water flowing out to its south, and now is connected to the Marshfield side and has water flowing out to its north.

The South River, formerly the last stretch of the North River, is the star of the view from Central Avenue on Humarock. To get there, cross the Sea Street Bridge, just south of the site of White's Ferry, and take a left. As you drive northward, remember that the old Pilgrim trail that ran toward Boston crossed at White's Ferry and continued up the peninsula. And why not? Rather than working all the way through the Marshfield Hills to find the crossing at Doggett's Ferry or Little's Bridge, one could walk over the shingle dike between Third and Fourth Cliffs and find the settlement on Kent Street in Scituate along the way.

The South River flows silently along as you continue to drive north before reaching the turnaround point at the fork with Beach Road. Look to the right for the open lot of land. That's where the Fourth Cliff Life-Saving Station stood until in burned down in 1919.

It's possible from here to put yourself in the shoes of the old river pilots. Imagine standing on the deck of the *Romulus* or the *Resolution*, or the *Diligence*, built in Smith's Yard near the North River Bridge in what was then Scituate (now Norwell). You've hollered out your navigation instructions for several days to reach this point, but that darned barrier beach stands in your way. You can even see the ocean breaking beyond the sands, but you now have to turn to starboard and continue your journey to the southeast.

Back to reality. Head south in your car and drive until you find Old Mouth Road to the south. You'll travel for more than two and a half miles, back past the Sea Street Bridge, past the Humarock Post Office, past the Julian Street Bridge, before coming across it. Imagine that here, somewhere, the river is finally flowing out to sea. And that it was not doing so reliably. The mouth kept shifting as the water moved the sand for the purpose of its own, naturally determined edification. Perhaps now you can see why the local shipbuilders fought so strongly for that canal between Third and Fourth Cliffs.

Whether it's raining or not, a drive along the banks of the North and South Rivers is well worth the day's excursion. The only thing that might have been better was to have stood on the deck of one of those schooners or brigs and seen it all from the pilot's point of view.

POSTSCRIPT

S o, after this journey through the history of the North River Valley, or at least those points that are accessible to the public, have we learned anything at all about which view of the river is best?

Is it the view from the Scituate shore, as seen by Samuel Deane and Harvey Hunter Pratt? Or from the Marshfield side, described by Lysander Richards and Joseph C. Hagar? Do we need a full end-to-end view, like one taken by L. Vernon Briggs, Joseph Foster Merritt or William Gould Vinal?

The fact remains that anyone who has ever written about the North River has held hopes and dreams for its future, and equally as vivid dreams of its past, no matter what his vantage point:

"North River may yet see another vessel, and perhaps many more built upon her banks. Several of the old shipbuilders affirm that in building small vessels there are no obstacles but what could easily be overcome, if the men had the courage." L. Vernon Briggs, *History of Shipbuilding on North River*, 1889

"A stranger standing in some deserted yard and reading the tablet, if he could also know the story of each vessel that was built there, where she sailed and in what distant sea or on what rugged coast she finally laid her bones, could gain some slight conception of the glory of a by-gone day." Joseph Foster Merritt, *Anecdotes of the North River and South Shore*, 1928

"The local laws have been changed in order to protect the disappearing shore birds. Is it possible that the North River country should now be a wildlife sanctuary and State Reservation?" William Gould Vinal, *Salt Haying in North River Valley (1648–1898)*, 1953

"The Indian spirit lingers here when the mist lies over the marshes, or when the great horned owl hunts silently along the marsh at night." Cynthia Hagar Krusell and Betty Magoun Bates, *Marshfield: A Town of Villages*, 1990

Vinal asks,

Where else can you stand with one foot in Pilgrim land and the other foot in Puritan land? Where else would you experience northeasters (one a generation) that change rivers, salt meadows and human life? Where else is there a garden of nature reserved for grasses, sea lavender, wild fowl, bivalves and humans? Where else are there islands surrounded by salt marshes? Where else are Anglo Saxon customs, speech, and freedom so well sealed away from the world? Where else have haycocks, gundalows, shipyards, bags of ducks, clambakes and freedoms of the beaches gone with the Northeast winds?

Is it possible that the American people, having worked so hard to gain freedom, are gradually becoming calloused, or indifferent to, the secrets of their achievements? How can we point out to our visiting friends the greatness of the present North River marshes if we are not truly aware ourselves?

In the end, the most important view of the river is the one that you, as an active citizen supporting conservation and preservation, choose to take. Perhaps you support the goals of just one of the many organizations mentioned in this book; perhaps you support several, but are opposed to the practices of others; maybe you support them all.

The history of the North River community can be explored in numerous places, in books tucked away on library shelves, in historical society exhibits and on the plaques marking the sites of shipyards of yore. The natural beauty of the North River is more tangible with every step one takes onto the trails of the many wildlife sanctuaries, memorial forests and reservations that line its banks and with every turn of a kayak paddle as one glides past Blueberry Island. The future of the North River, the one that our children, grandchildren and great-grandchildren will know, is in the palms of our own hands right now.

If any portion of this book has stirred your interest in the future of the river, take action. Walk the trails; partake of the North and South Rivers through all of your senses; cherish them for what they are, what they have provided and what they represent; and join the thousands of others invested in carrying on the legacies of Cornet Robert Stetson, Edward Wanton, Henry W. Nelson and everybody who loved the river before we came along. Every dollar donated and every hour volunteered assures a better future for us all.

Appendix

Visiting the North River

Thanks to the persistent efforts of the nonprofit organizations mentioned in this book, the North River Commission, the State of Massachusetts and the town governments of the North River communities, not to mention the many private citizens who have donated time, money and sweat equity to conservation efforts along the North and South Rivers' banks, there are numerous places to enjoy their natural and historical beauty.

The following list only includes open space parcels that directly abut the rivers, and a few historic sites along their banks. The full story of the rivers, though, reaches out to its entire watershed, and there are more places to go to visit the many millponds and streams that feed the main rivers. Luckily for us all, the North and South Rivers Watershed Association has published a comprehensive map listing and locating 118 points of natural or historical interest in the watershed. Purchase one (proceeds support the association's activities) before you head out on your next walk, and you'll see that there's much, much more to the river than you ever thought there was.

Walking Trails

Hanover

Luddam's Ford Park, Hanover Conservation Commission
22 acres, meadow and forest
Directions from Route 3 South: Take Exit 13 for Route 53 and follow Route 53 South. Travel south for three miles to Broadway. Take a right onto Broadway, and then bear left onto Elm Street. Luddam's Ford Park is on the right.
www.hanover-ma.gov

Marshfield

Two Mile Reservation, Trustees of Reservations
68 acres, woodlands

Directions from Route 3 South: Take Exit 12 and follow Route 139 South toward Marshfield. Take a left at Union Street and watch for the entrance to Two Mile Reservation on the left.
www.thetrustees.org

Cornhill Woodland, Town of Marshfield
123 acres, woodlands, salt marsh, freshwater wetlands
Directions from Route 3 South: Take Exit 12 and follow Route 139 South toward Marshfield. Take a left at Union Street and follow that for two and a half miles to Cornhill Lane. Take a left on Cornhill Lane and follow it to the end, being careful around a tight turn as the road slopes down to the river valley, to park in the cul-de-sac. Enjoy the view. Walk back up the street and watch for the opening to Cornhill Woodlands on the left.
www.townofmarshfield.org

Henry and Thomas Nelson Memorial Forest, New England Forestry Foundation
130 acres, woods, leading to a packet landing on the North River
Directions from Route 3 South: Take Exit 12 and follow Route 139 South toward Marshfield. Take a left at Union Street and follow that for two and a half miles, bearing right onto Highland Street. Go up and over the crest of the hill, past open farmland on the right and watch for a dirt road on the left that looks like a driveway. Parking is just behind the tree line.
www.neforestry.org/forestry/forestdetail.asp?id=9

North River Wildlife Sanctuary, Mass Audubon
180 acres, woodlands, grasslands, overlook on North River
Directions from Route 3 South: Take Exit 12 and follow Route 139 South toward Marshfield. Take a left at Union Street and follow that for two and a half miles, bearing right onto Highland Street. Follow Highland Street for a mile and turn left on Spring Street. Follow Spring Street to its intersection with Route 3A. Turn right on Route 3A and watch immediately for the entrance to the North River Wildlife Sanctuary on the left.
www.massaudubon.org/northriver

Bridle Path, Town of Marshfield
3 mile former railroad bed, crosses the South River
Directions from Route 3 South: Take Exit 12 and follow Route 139 South toward Marshfield for three and a half miles. Park in the CVS Pharmacy parking lot across from the head of Webster Street. The Bridle Path opens behind the parking lot.
www.townofmarshfield.org/Public_Documents/MarshfieldMA_Conservation

Norwell

Stetson Meadows, Town of Norwell
47 acres, woods

Directions from Route 3 South: Take Exit 13 and follow Route 53 South for three miles. Take a left at Broadway, continue across the intersection onto River Street. Take a right on Stetson Shrine Lane and follow that onto Meadow Farms Way. Follow the dirt road into the woods, taking a left in front of the old farmhouse to find the parking lot for Stetson Meadows.
www.norwellma.com

Albert Norris Reservation and McMullan Woods, Trustees of Reservations
129 acres of woods, with extensive river frontage
Directions from Route 3 South: Take Exit 13 and follow Route 53 North to Route 123. Turn right on Route 123, Webster Street, for three and a half miles. Pass through Norwell center and take a right on Dover Street. The parking area for Norris Reservation is on the left.
www.thetrustees.org

Pembroke

Tucker Preserve, Wildlands Trust of Southeastern Massachusetts
78.6 acres, woods
Directions from Route 3 South: Take Exit 13 for Route 53 and follow Route 53 South. Travel south for three miles to Broadway. Take a right onto Broadway, and then bear left onto Elm Street. Pass the entrance to Luddam's Ford Park and park in the town-owned lot on the left. Trails can be accessed through the adjoining town land.
www.wildlandstrust.org

Scituate

Driftway Conservation Park, Town of Scituate
450 acres, salt marsh and views of the Herring River
Directions from Route 3 South: Take Exit 13 and follow Route 53 North to Route 123. Turn right on Route 123, Webster Street. Follow Route 123 to its terminus in Scituate at the Greenbush rotary. Take the second right off the rotary onto the Driftway. Follow that past the Scituate Maritime & Irish Mossing Museum and watch for the Driftway Conservation Park parking lot on the left.
www.town.scituate.ma.us

Canoe Launches

The North and South Rivers Watershed Association's Paddling Guide is available as a downloadable pdf document at www.nsrwa.org/pdf/kayakguidebook.pdf. For important safety information and more detailed information on canoeing or kayaking the rivers, please download and read the eleven-page guide. Please note that kayaking and canoeing are not advisable east of the Route 3A Bridge due to swift-moving currents and the dangerous area around the mouth of the North and South Rivers.

Hanover

Hanover Canoe Launch
Above the Crotch, the confluence of the Indian Head River and the Herring River where the North River is formed
Directions from Route 3 South: Take Exit 13 for Route 53 and follow Route 53 South. Travel south for three miles to Broadway. Take a right onto Broadway, and then bear left onto Elm Street. Take a left on Indian Head Drive. The canoe launch is at the end of the road on the right.

Marshfield

Marshfield Canoe Launch
South of the Union Street Bridge
Directions from Route 3 South: Take Exit 13 and follow Route 53 North to Route 123. Turn right on Route 123, Webster Street, for four miles. Pass through Norwell center and take a right on Bridge Street. Cross the bridge and immediately watch for a driveway to the right at the site of the Brooks-Tilden Shipyard.

Norwell

Chittenden Lane Canoe Launch
At the end of Chittenden Lane, limited parking
Directions from Route 3 South: Take Exit 13 and follow Route 53 South for three miles. Take a left at Broadway and continue across the intersection onto River Street. Follow River Street to Chittenden Lane. Take a right on Chittenden Lane and follow to the end. When you launch, keep in mind that this site was where the *Helen M. Foster*, the last ship built on the North River, launched from in 1871.

Norwell Boat Launch
North of the Union Street Bridge, resident sticker required for parking
Directions from Route 3 South: Take Exit 13 and follow Route 53 North to Route 123. Turn right on Route 123, Webster Street, for four miles. Pass through Norwell center and take a right on Bridge Street. The bridge will appear after approximately one-third of a mile. The parking lot is on the left.

King's Landing Marina
North of Union Bridge, canoe rentals
Directions from Route 3 South: Take Exit 13 and follow Route 53 North to Route 123. Turn right on Route 123, Webster Street, for four and a half miles. Turn right on King's Landing and watch for the marina.

Pembroke

Pembroke Canoe Launch
On Brick Kiln Lane, east of the confluence of Third Herring Brook and the North River
Directions from Route 3 South: Take Exit 13 for Route 53 and follow Route 53 South.
Travel south for four miles to Schoosett Street. Take a left onto Schoosett Street and a
left onto Brick Kiln Lane. Follow Brick Kiln Lane as it winds around past a llama pen.
Watch for a dirt driveway on the right. The canoe launch site is at the end of the road.

Please refer to the *NSRWA Canoe and Kayak Guide* for information about launch sites on
the South River.

Places to Learn More

Hanover

Hanover Historical Society
514 Hanover Street
P.O. Box 156
Hanover, MA 02339
www.hanover-ma.gov

Friends of the Stetson House, Inc.
514 Hanover Street
P.O. Box 2064
Hanover, MA 02339
781.826.9575
www.hanover-ma.gov

Marshfield

Marshfield Historical Society
Webster and Careswell Streets
P.O. Box 1244
Marshfield, MA 02050
www.marshfieldhistoricalsociety.com

Mass Audubon
North River Wildlife Sanctuary
2000 Main Street
Marshfield, MA 02050
781.837.9400
www.massaudubon.org/northriver

Winslow House Association
634 Careswell Street
Marshfield, MA 02050
781.837.5753
www.marshfield.net/winslow

Norwell

James Library and Center for the Arts
24 West Street
P.O. Box 164
Norwell, MA 02061
781.659.7100
www.firstparishnorwell.org

North and South Rivers Watershed Association
P.O. Box 43
Norwell, MA 02061
781.659.8168
www.nsrwa.org

Norwell Historical Society
328 Main Street
Norwell, MA 02061
781.659.1888

South Shore Natural Science Center
Jacobs Lane
Norwell, MA 02061
781.659.2259
www.ssnsc.org

Pembroke

Pembroke Historical Society
116 Center Street
P.O. Box 122
Pembroke, MA 02359
781.293.9083

Scituate

Scituate Historical Society
43 Cudworth Road
P.O. Box 276
Scituate, MA 02066
781.545.1083
www.scituatehistoricalsociety.org

Scituate Maritime & Irish Mossing Museum
301 Driftway
Scituate, MA 02066
www.scituatehistoricalsociety.org

BIBLIOGRAPHICAL ESSAY

The historian looking to research the story of the North River certainly has a daunting, unenviable task ahead of him or her. It's a job no one should wish upon another human being. There simply is so much information available that it's nearly impossible to pare it all down to a concentrated, cohesive work of written art.

Take, for starters, L. Vernon Briggs's *History of Shipbuilding on North River* (Boston: Coburn Brothers, 1889). It's 421 pages long! Briggs gathered an exhaustive amount of information on the shipbuilders and their families, making the book both a history and a genealogy. And it's the starting point for research on the history of the river. The Norwell Historical Society should be commended for reprinting this magnificent work of local history.

Joseph Foster Merritt's *Anecdotes of the North River and South Shore* (Rockland, MA: Rockland Standard Publishing Company, 1928) is an absolute treasure of local history as well, with short tales on numerous topics, most of which revolve around life on the river.

Community histories of the major adjoining towns form a special collection of books that must be referenced when researching the river. Hanover offers John Stetson Barry's *A Historical Sketch of the Town of Hanover, Massachusetts, with family genealogies* (S.G. Drake, 1853); *History of the Town of Hanover, Massachusetts* (Hanover, MA, 1910) by Jedediah Dwelley; *A History of the Town of Hanover, Massachusetts, 1910 to 1977* (Hanover, MA: Hanover Historical Society, 1977) by Fanny Hitchcock Phillips; and Barbara Underwood Barker's *Houses of the Revolution in Hanover, Massachusetts* (Hanover, MA: Hanover Historical Society, 1976). Barbara Barker's "Focus on History" articles on Hanover, online at www.hanover-ma.gov/pdf/forms/historical/Hanover-Focus-On-History.pdf, are a wonderful resource for the history of that town. Neighboring Pembroke has published commemorative histories on the town's 250th (1962) and 275th (1987) anniversaries, and the country's bicentennial (1976). William Walter Bryant wrote *Historic Pembroke, 1712–1912* (Bryantville, MA: Bryantville News, 1912) for the town's centennial celebration.

The Norwell Historical Society published *Historical Homesteads of Norwell, Massachusetts* (Norwell, MA: Norwell Historical Society, 1992) and reprinted Joseph Foster Merritt's

1938 *A Narrative History of South Scituate-Norwell, Massachusetts* (Norwell, MA: Norwell Historical Society, 1987).

Scituate may be the most prolific town on the South Shore. One of the most important works for the purposes of this book was Samuel L. Deane's *History of Scituate, 1831* (Boston: James Loring, 1831). Reverend Deane, who lived a century and a half closer to the early settlers of the river than any of us alive today, provides several family histories in the back half of his book, which are expanded upon by Harvey Hunter Pratt in *Early Planters of Scituate* (Scituate, MA: Scituate Historical Society, 1929). Pratt also penned an important small work, *The Harbor at Scituate, Massachusetts*, recently reprinted by the Scituate Historical Society. Scituate also compiled commemorative histories for the 300th (1936) and 325th (1961) anniversaries, and the Chief Justice Cushing Chapter of the Daughters of the American Revolution pulled together *Old Scituate* in 1921, reprinted in 2000 by the DAR and the Scituate Historical Society. While many books have been written about the Pilgrims and their experiences in the New World, only one truly focuses on the life of Scituate's first citizen, and that's Stephen R. Valdespino's *Timothy Hatherly and the Plymouth Colony Pilgrims* (Scituate, MA: Scituate Historical Society, 1987).

David Ball and Fred Freitas have published several books about shipwrecks and maritime history on the South Shore, and none is more important to this work than *Warnings Ignored! The Story of the Portland Gale, November 1898* (Scituate, MA: self-published, 1995). This book led the way for the publication of Mason Philip Smith and Peter Dow Batchelder's *Four Short Blasts: The Gale of 1898 and the Loss of the Steamer Portland* (Portland, ME: The Provincial Press, 2003). Together these books entail the best out there on the Portland Gale, the storm that changed the course of the North River.

Marshfield's contributions come in three major time periods. First, Lysander Salmon Richards's *History of Marshfield* (Plymouth, MA: Memorial Press, 1901) offers details not found elsewhere about attempts to dig new channels through Humarock and between Third and Fourth Cliffs to manually change the course of the North and South Rivers. Joseph C. Hagar's *Marshfield: The Autobiography of a Pilgrim Town* (Marshfield, MA: Marshfield Tercentenary Committee, 1940) served as the town's tercentennial history. The pièce de résistance for Marshfield, though, is Cynthia Hagar Krusell and Betty Magoun Bates's *Marshfield: A Town of Villages* (Marshfield Hills, MA: Historical Research Associates, 1990), a remarkable book that never seems to age, even nearly two decades removed from its publication.

Arcadia Publishing's *Images of America* pictorial histories offer quick snapshots of local history intended to help whet a novice historian's appetite. Most of the towns in the region have published them. *Hanover* (Charleston, SC: Arcadia, 2004) was completed by Barbara Underhill Barker and Les Molyneaux. James Pierotti wrote *Norwell* (Charleston, SC: Arcadia, 2005); *Scituate* (Charleston, SC: Arcadia, 2000) was a team effort by David Ball, Fred Freitas, John Galluzzo and Carol Miles; while *Then & Now: Scituate* (Charleston, SC: Arcadia, 2002) was a collaboration of David Corbin and John Galluzzo. *Marshfield* (Charleston, SC: Arcadia, 2007) was coauthored by Cynthia Hagar Krusell and John Galluzzo. Galluzzo also wrote *Mass Audubon* (Charleston, SC: Arcadia, 2003), which includes a chapter on both the North River and Daniel Webster Wildlife Sanctuaries.

Several ancillary studies have been referenced for this history to come alive. Gerald W. Butler's *The Guns of Boston Harbor* (Bloomington, IN: 1st Books, 2001) extensively covers the military history of Fourth Cliff. Ralph Shanks, Lisa Woo Shanks and Wick York's *The United States Life-Saving Service: Heroes, Rescues and Architecture of the Early Coast Guard* (Petaluma, CA: Costano Books, 1995) gives an overview of that service and details on the Fourth Cliff station. William H. Marnell's *Vacation Yesterdays of New England* (New York: Seabury Press, 1975) covers the history of vacationing on the South Shore of Boston, with a particular focus on the Marshfield and Scituate coastlines. Fessenden S. Blanchard went so far as to classify the North River as one of his *Ghost Towns of New England* (New York: Dodd, Mead & Company, 1961). Benjamin Woods Labaree's *The Boston Tea Party* (Boston: Northeastern University Press, 1964) covers the story of that infamous event, which featured the North River–built brig *Beaver*. Robert M. Thorson's *Stone By Stone: The Magnificent History in New England's Stone Walls* (New York: Walker and Company, 2002) lovingly covers the topic it describes

Three books have been written about one particular ship built on the North River, or rather, about the grisly mutiny that occurred on it: Edwin P. Hoyt's *Mutiny on the Globe* (Guilford, CT: The Lyons Press, 1975); Thomas Farel Heffernan's *Mutiny on the Globe: The Fatal Voyage of Samuel Comstock* (New York: W.W. Norton & Co., 2002); and Gregory Gibson's *Demon of the Waters* (Boston: Little, Brown & Company, 2002). The latter title gives an excellent description of the various phases of construction of a North River ship, from contract to tree selection to launch.

One article in particular jumped out as needing to be included in this essay, that being Paul Huffington and J. Nelson Clifford's "Evolution of Shipbuilding in Southeastern Massachusetts" in *Economic Geography* 15, no. 4 (October 1939), 362–78. A post-Briggs and unattached study of shipbuilding on the North River, it explores areas that Briggs either couldn't or wouldn't go.

Dozens of online genealogical resources were checked to cross-reference birth, marriage and death information found in the books listed above, sometimes to the detriment of the author, as not every vital record lined up with military precision in both its digital and printed forms.

Historical ornithological information was drawn primarily from two sources, Edward Howe Forbush's *Birds of Massachusetts and Other New England States*, published in three volumes (Boston: Massachusetts Department of Agriculture, 1925–1929) and Arthur Cleveland Bent's various *Life Histories of North American Birds* (Washington, D.C.: U.S. Government Printing Office, 1921–1968). Even if you're not into birds, these books are simply fun to read in part for the odd slices of Americana they serve up.

The *North River Management Plan (and Regulations)*, published in July 1980 by the Massachusetts Department of Environmental Management, is a document every abutter to the river should own and know by heart. Most of the towns in the region have either an open space or conservation map available for free at their respective town halls, and the North and South River Watershed Association's *North and South Rivers Guide* is an outstanding piece of work in itself, part map, part history. The association also published the important *NSRWA Canoe and Kayak Guide* downloadable from the NSRWA website, www.nsrwa.org.

Finally, no study of the North River can be called remotely complete without finding out what William Gould Vinal had to say about the topic. Professor of nature education, champion of the movement to keep kids outside and an honorary vice-president of the Massachusetts Audubon Society, Vinal's *Salt-haying in the North River Valley (1648–1898)* (Norwell, MA: Norwell Historical Society, 1953) is the perfect blend of memory, research and anecdote on the topic. His approach was unique and his determination for kids to learn from being outdoors and free to roam was unbounded. The world needs more William Gould Vinals. Also, his *South Shore, New and Old: A Medley of Historical Facts and Places* (Chief Justice Cushing Chapter, Scituate, MA: Daughters of the American Revolution, 1975) offers an excellent glossary of terms only to be found on the North River.

Various other publications have been referred to and cited in the text for information as obscure as radio direction finding, cosmic ray research and the English Civil War as they pertained to the history of the North River.